PENGUIN BOOKS — GREAT IDEAS

Of Man

Thomas Hobbes
1588–1679

Thomas Hobbes

Of Man

PENGUIN BOOKS — GREAT IDEAS

PENGUIN BOOKS

Published by the Penguin Group
Penguin Books Ltd, 80 Strand, London WC2R ORL, England
Penguin Group (USA) Inc., 375 Hudson Street, New York, New York 10014, USA
Penguin Group (Canada), 10 Alcorn Avenue, Toronto, Ontario, Canada M4V 3B2
(a division of Pearson Penguin Canada Inc.)
Penguin Ireland, 25 St Stephen's Green, Dublin 2, Ireland
(a division of Penguin Books Ltd)
Penguin Group (Australia), 250 Camberwell Road,
Camberwell, Victoria 3124, Australia (a division of Pearson Australia Group Pty Ltd)
Penguin Books India Pvt Ltd, 11 Community Centre,
Panchsheel Park, New Delhi – 110 017, India
Penguin Group (NZ), cnr Airborne and Rosedale Roads, Albany,
Auckland 1310, New Zealand (a division of Pearson New Zealand Ltd)
Penguin Books (South Africa) (Pty) Ltd, 24 Sturdee Avenue,
Rosebank 2196, South Africa

Penguin Books Ltd, Registered Offices: 80 Strand, London WC2R ORL, England

www.penguin.com

Leviathan first published 1651
First published in Penguin Classics 1985
This extract published in Penguin Books 2005

1

Taken from the Penguin Classics edition of *Leviathan*,
edited by C. B. MacPherson

Set by Rowland Phototypesetting Ltd, Bury St Edmunds, Suffolk
Printed in England by Clays Ltd, St Ives plc

Contents

The Introduction

Nature (the Art whereby God hath made and governes the World) is by the *Art* of man, as in many other things, so in this also imitated, that it can make an Artificial Animal. For seeing life is but a motion of Limbs, the begining whereof is in some principall part within; why may we not say, that all *Automata* (Engines that move themselves by springs and wheeles as doth a watch) have an artificiall life? For what is the *Heart*, but a *Spring*; and the *Nerves*, but so many *Strings*; and the *Joynts*, but so many *Wheeles*, giving motion to the whole Body, such as was intended by the Artificer? *Art* goes yet further, imitating that Rationall and most excellent worke of Nature, *Man*. For by Art is created that great LEVIATHAN called a COMMON-WEALTH, or STATE, (in latine CIVITAS) which is but an Artificiall Man; though of greater stature and strength than the Naturall, for whose protection and defence it was intended; and in which, the *Soveraignty* is an Artificiall *Soul*, as giving life and motion to the whole body; The *Magistrates*, and other *Officers* of Judicature and Execution, artificiall *Joynts*; *Reward* and *Punishment* (by which fastned to the seate of the Soveraignty, every joynt and member is moved to performe his duty) are the *Nerves*, that do the same in the Body Naturall; The *Wealth* and *Riches* of all the particular members, are the *Strength*; *Salus Populi* (the *peoples safety*) its *Businesse*;

Counsellors, by whom all things needfull for it to know, are suggested unto it, are the *Memory*; *Equity* and *Lawes*, an artificiall *Reason* and *Will*; *Concord, Health*; *Sedition, Sickness*; and *Civill war, Death*. Lastly, the *Pacts* and *Covenants*, by which the parts of this Body Politique were at first made, set together, and united, resemble that *Fiat*, or the *Let us make man*, pronounced by God in the Creation.

To describe the Nature of this Artificiall man, I will consider

First, the *Matter* thereof, and the *Artificer*; both which is *Man*.

Secondly, *How*, and by what *Covenants* it is made; what are the *Rights* and just *Power* or *Authority* of a *Soveraigne*; and what it is that *preserveth* and *dissolveth* it.

Thirdly, what is a *Christian Common-wealth*.

Lastly, what is the *Kingdome of Darkness*.

Concerning the first, there is a saying much usurped of late, That *Wisedome* is acquired, not by reading of *Books*, but of *Men*. Consequently whereunto, those persons, that for the most part can give no other proof of being wise, take great delight to shew what they think they have read in men, by uncharitable censures of one another behind their backs. But there is another saying not of late understood, by which they might learn truly to read one another, if they would take the pains; and that is, *Nosce teipsum, Read thy self*: which was not meant, as it is now used, to countenance, either the barbarous state of men in power, towards their inferiors; or to encourage men of low degree, to a sawcie behaviour towards their betters; But to teach us, that for the similitude of the thoughts, and Passions of one man, to the thoughts, and Passions of another, whosoever looketh into himself, and considereth what he doth, when he does *think, opine, reason, hope, feare,* &c, and upon what grounds; he shall thereby read and know, what are the thoughts, and Passions of all other men, upon the like occasions. I say the similitude of *Passions,* which are the same in all men, *desire, feare, hope,* &c; not the similitude of *the objects* of the Passions, which are the things *desired, feared, hoped,* &c: for these the constitution individuall, and particular education do so vary, and they are so easie to be kept from our knowledge, that the characters of mans heart, blotted and confounded as they are, with dissembling, lying, counterfeiting, and erroneous doctrines, are legible onely to him that searcheth hearts. And though by mens actions wee do discover their designe sometimes; yet to do it without comparing them with our own, and distinguishing all circumstances, by which the case may come to be altered, is to decypher without a key, and be for the most part deceived, by too much trust, or by too much diffidence; as he that reads, is himself a good or evil man.

But let one man read another by his actions never so perfectly, it serves him onely with his acquaintance, which are but few. He that is to govern a whole Nation, must read in himself, not this, or that particular man; but Man-kind: which though it be hard to do, harder than to learn any Language, or Science; yet, when I shall have set down my own reading orderly, and perspicuously, the pains left another, will be onely to consider, if he also find not the same in himself. For this kind of Doctrine, admitteth no other Demonstration.

Of Man

Of SENSE

Concerning the Thoughts of man, I will consider them first *Singly*, and afterwards in *Trayne*, or dependance upon one another. *Singly*, they are every one a *Representation* or *Apparence*, of some quality, or other Accident of a body without us; which is commonly called an *Object*. Which Object worketh on the Eyes, Eares, and other parts of mans body; and by diversity of working, produceth diversity of Apparences.

The Originall of them all, is that which we call SENSE; (For there is no conception in a mans mind, which hath not at first, totally, or by parts, been begotten upon the organs of Sense.) The rest are derived from that originall.

To know the naturall cause of Sense, is not very necessary to the business now in hand; and I have elsewhere written of the same at large. Nevertheless, to fill each part of my present method, I will briefly deliver the same in this place.

The cause of Sense, is the Externall Body, or Object, which presseth the organ proper to each Sense, either immediatly, as in the Tast and Touch; or mediately, as in Seeing, Hearing, and Smelling: which pressure, by the mediation of Nerves, and other strings, and membranes of the body, continued inwards to the Brain, and Heart, causeth there a resistance, or counter-pressure, or endeavour of the heart, to deliver it self: which endeavour because *Outward*, seemeth to be some matter without. And this *seeming*, or *fancy*, is that which men call *Sense*; and consisteth, as to the Eye, in a *Light*, or *Colour figured*; To the Eare, in a *Sound*; To the Nostrill, in an *Odour*; To the Tongue and Palat, in a *Savour*; And to the rest of the body, in *Heat, Cold, Hardnesse, Softnesse*, and such other qualities, as we discern by *Feeling*. All which qualities called *Sensible*, are in the object that causeth them, but so many several motions of the matter, by which it presseth our organs diversly. Neither in us that are pressed, are they anything else, but divers motions; (for motion, produceth nothing but motion.) But their apparence to us is Fancy, the same waking, that dreaming. And as pressing, rubbing, or striking the Eye, makes us fancy a light; and pressing the Eare, produceth a dinne; so do the bodies also wee see, or hear, produce the same by their strong, though unobserved action. For if those Colours, and Sounds, were in the Bodies, or Objects that cause them, they could not bee severed from them, as by glasses, and in Ecchoes by reflection, wee see they are; where we know the thing we see, is in one place; the apparence, in another. And though at some certain distance, the reall, and very object seem invested with the fancy it begets in us; Yet still the object is one thing, the image or fancy is another. So that Sense in all cases, is nothing els but originall fancy, caused (as I have said) by the pressure, that is, by the motion, of externall things upon our Eyes, Eares, and other organs thereunto ordained.

But the Philosophy-schooles, through all the Universities of Christendome, grounded upon certain Texts of *Aristotle*, teach another doctrine; and say, For the cause of *Vision*, that the thing seen, sendeth forth on every side a *visible species* (in English) a *visible shew, apparition*, or *aspect*, or *a being seen*; the receiving whereof into the Eye, is *Seeing*. And for the cause of *Hearing*, that the thing heard, sendeth forth an *Audible species*, that is, an *Audible aspect*, or *Audible being seen*; which entring at the Eare, maketh *Hearing*. Nay for the cause of *Understanding* also, they say the thing Understood sendeth forth *intelligible species*, that is, an *intelligible being seen*; which comming into the Understanding, makes us Understand. I say not this, as disapproving the use of Universities: but because I am to speak hereafter of their office in a Commonwealth, I must let you see on all occasions by the way, what things would be amended in them; amongst which the frequency of insignificant Speech is one.

Of IMAGINATION

That when a thing lies still, unlesse somewhat els stirre it, it will lye still for ever, is a truth that no man doubts of. But that when a thing is in motion, it will eternally be in motion, unless somewhat els stay it, though the reason be the same, (namely, that nothing can change it selfe,) is not so easily assented to. For men measure, not onely other men, but all other things, by themselves: and because they find themselves subject after motion to pain, and lassitude, think every thing els growes weary of motion, and seeks repose of its own accord; little considering, whether it be not some other motion, wherein that desire of rest they find in themselves, consisteth. From hence it is, that the Schooles say, Heavy bodies fall downwards, out of an appetite to rest, and to conserve their nature in that place which is most proper for them; ascribing appetite, and Knowledge of what is good for their conservation, (which is more than man has) to things inanimate absurdly.

When a Body is once in motion, it moveth (unless something els hinder it) eternally; and whatsoever hindreth it, cannot in an instant, but in time, and by degrees quite extinguish it: And as wee see in the water, though the wind cease, the waves give not over rowling for a long time after; so also it happeneth in that motion, which is made in the internall parts of a man, then, when he Sees, Dreams, &c. For after the object is removed, or the eye shut, wee still retain an image of the thing seen, though more obscure than when we see it. And this is it, the Latines call *Imagination*, from the image made in seeing; and apply the same, though improperly, to all the other senses. But the Greeks call it *Fancy*; which signifies *apparence*, and is as proper to one sense, as to another. IMAGINATION therefore is nothing but *decaying sense*; and is found in men, and many other living Creatures, as well sleeping, as waking.

The decay of Sense in men waking, is not the decay of the motion made in sense; but an obscuring of it, in such manner, as the light of the Sun obscureth the light of the Starres; which starrs do no less exercise their vertue by which they are visible, in the day, than in the night. But because amongst many stroaks, which our eyes, eares, and other organs receive from externall bodies, the predominant onely is sensible; therefore the light of the Sun being predominant, we are not affected with the action of the starrs. And any object being removed from our eyes, though the impression it made in us remain; yet other objects more present succeeding, and working on us, the Imagination of the past is obscured, and made weak; as the voyce of a man is in the noyse of the day. From whence it followeth, that the longer the time is, after the sight, or Sense of any object, the weaker is the Imagination. For the continuall change of mans body, destroyes in time the parts which in sense were moved: So that distance of time, and of place, hath one and the same effect in us. For as at a distance of place, that which wee look at, appears dimme, and without distinction of the smaller parts; and as Voyces grow weak, and inarticulate: so also after great distance of time, our imagination of the Past is weak; and wee lose (for example) of Cities wee have seen, many particular Streets; and of Actions, many particular Circumstances. This *decaying sense*, when wee would express the thing it self, (I mean *fancy* it selfe,) wee call *Imagination*, as I said before: But when we would express the *decay*, and signifie that the Sense is fading, old, and past, it is called *Memory*. So that *Imagination* and *Memory*, are but one thing, which for divers considerations hath divers names.

Much memory, or memory of many things, is called *Experience*. Againe, Imagination being only of those things which have been formerly perceived by Sense, either all at once, or by parts at severall times; The former, (which is the imagining the whole object, as it was presented to the sense) is *simple Imagination*; as when one imagineth a man, or horse, which he hath seen before. The other is *Compounded*; as when from the sight of a man at one time, and of a horse at another, we conceive in our mind a Centaure. So when a man compoundeth the image of his own person, with the image of the actions of an other man; as when a man imagins himselfe a *Hercules*, or an *Alexander*, (which happeneth often to them that are much taken with reading of Romants) it is a compound imagination, and properly but a Fiction of the mind. There be also other Imaginations that rise in men, (though waking) from the great impression made in sense: As from gazing upon the Sun, the impression leaves an image of the Sun before our eyes a long time after; and from being long and vehemently attent upon Geometricall Figures, a man shall in the dark, (though awake) have the Images of Lines, and Angles before his eyes: which kind of Fancy hath no particular name; as being a thing that doth not commonly fall into mens discourse.

The imaginations of them that sleep, are those we call *Dreams*. And these also (as all other Imaginations) have been before, either totally, or by parcells in the Sense. And because in sense, the Brain, and Nerves, which are the necessary Organs of sense, are so benummed in sleep, as not easily to be moved by the action of Externall Objects, there can happen in sleep, no Imagination; and therefore no Dreame, but what proceeds from the agitation of the inward parts of mans body; which inward parts, for the connexion they have with the Brayn, and other Organs, when they be distempered, do keep the same in motion; whereby the Imaginations there formerly made, appeare as if a man were waking; saving that the Organs of Sense being now benummed, so as there is no new object, which can master and obscure them with a more vigorous impression, a Dreame must needs be more cleare, in this silence of sense, than are our waking thoughts. And hence it cometh to passe, that it is a hard matter, and by many thought impossible to distinguish exactly between Sense and Dreaming. For my part, when I consider, that in Dreames, I do not often, nor constantly think of the same Persons, Places, Objects, and Actions that I do waking; nor remember so long a trayne of coherent thoughts, Dreaming, as at other times; And because waking I often observe the absurdity of Dreames, but never dream of the absurdities of my waking Thoughts; I am well satisfied, that being awake, I know I dreame not; though when I dreame, I think my selfe awake.

And seeing dreames are caused by the distemper of some of the inward parts of the Body; divers distempers must needs cause different Dreams. And hence it is, that lying cold breedeth Dreams of Feare, and raiseth the thought and Image of some fearfull object (the motion from the brain to the inner parts, and from the inner parts to the Brain being reciprocall:) And that as Anger causeth heat in some parts of the Body, when we are awake; so when we sleep, the over heating of the same parts causeth Anger, and raiseth up in the brain the Imagination of an Enemy. In the same manner; as natu- rall kindness, when we are awake causeth desire; and desire makes heat in certain other parts of the body; so also, too much heat in those parts, while wee sleep, raiseth in the brain an imagination of some kindness shewn. In summe, our Dreams are the reverse of our waking Imaginations; The motion when we are awake, beginning at one end; and when we Dream, at another.

The most difficult discerning of a mans Dream, from his waking thoughts, is then, when by some accident we observe not that we have slept: which is easie to happen to a man full of fearfull thoughts; and whose conscience is much troubled; and that sleepeth, without the circumstances, of going to bed, or putting off his clothes, as one that noddeth in a chayre. For he that taketh pains, and industriously layes himself to sleep, in case any uncouth and exorbitant fancy come unto him, cannot easily think it other than a Dream. We read of *Marcus Brutus*, (one that had his life given him by *Julius Cæsar*, and was also his favorite, and notwithstanding murthered him,) how at *Philippi*, the night before he gave battell to *Augustus Cæsar*, hee saw a fearfull apparition, which is commonly related by Historians as a Vision: but considering the circumstances, one may easily judge to have been but a short Dream. For sitting in his tent, pensive and troubled with the horrour of his rash act, it was not hard for him, slumbering in the cold, to dream of that which most affrighted him; which feare, as by degrees it made him wake; so also it must needs make the Apparition by degrees to vanish: And having no assurance that he slept, he could have no cause to think it a Dream, or any thing but a Vision. And this is no very rare Accident: for even they that be perfectly awake, if they be timorous, and supperstitious, possessed with fearfull tales, and alone in the dark, are subject to the like fancies, and believe they see spirits and dead mens Ghosts walking in Church-yards; whereas it is either their Fancy onely, or els the knavery of such persons, as make use of such super-stitious feare, to passe disguised in the night, to places they would not be known to haunt.

From this ignorance of how to distinguish Dreams, and other strong Fancies, from Vision and Sense, did arise the greatest part of the Religion of the Gentiles in time past, that worshipped Satyres, Fawnes, Nymphs, and the like; and now adayes the opinion that rude people have of Fayries, Ghosts, and Goblins; and of the power of Witches. For as for Witches, I think not that their witchcraft is any reall power; but yet that they are justly punished, for the false beliefe they have, that they can do such mischiefe, joyned with their purpose to do it if they can: their trade being neerer to a new Religion, than to a Craft or Science. And for Fayries, and walking Ghosts, the opinion of them has I think been on purpose, either taught, or not confuted, to keep in credit the use of Exorcisme, of Crosses, of holy Water, and other such inventions of Ghostly men. Neverthelesse, there is no doubt, but God can make unnaturall Apparitions: But that he does it so often, as men need to feare such things, more than they feare the stay, or change, of the course of Nature, which he also can stay, and change, is no point of Christian faith. But evill men under pretext that God can do any thing, are so bold as to say any thing when it serves their turn, though they think it untrue; It is the part of a wise man, to believe them no further, than right reason makes that which they say, appear credible. If this superstitious fear of Spirits were taken away, and with it, Prognostiques from Dreams, false Prophecies, and many other things depending thereon, by which, crafty ambitious persons abuse the simple people, men would be much more fitted than they are for civill Obedience.

And this ought to be the work of the Schooles: but they rather nourish such doctrine. For (not knowing what Imagination, or the Senses are), what they receive, they teach: some saying, that Imaginations rise of themselves, and have no cause: Others that they rise most commonly from the Will; and that Good thoughts are blown (inspired) into a man, by God; and Evill thoughts by the Divell: or that Good thoughts are powred (infused) into a man, by God, and Evill ones by the Divell. Some say the Senses receive the Species of things, and deliver them to the Common-sense; and the Common Sense delivers them over to the Fancy, and the Fancy to the Memory, and the Memory to the Judgement, like handing of things from one to another, with many words making nothing understood.

The Imagination that is raysed in man (or any other creature indued with the faculty of imagining) by words, or other voluntary signes, is that we generally call *Understanding*; and is common to Man and Beast. For a dogge by custome will understand the call, or the rating of his Master; and so will many other Beasts. That Understanding which is peculiar to man, is the Understanding not onely his will; but his conceptions and thoughts, by the sequell and contexture of the names of things into Affirmations, Negations, and other formes of Speech: And of this kinde of Understanding I shall speak hereafter.

Of the Consequence or TRAYNE *of Imaginations*

By *Consequence*, or TRAYNE of Thoughts, I understand that succession of one Thought to another, which is called (to distinguish it from Discourse in words) *Mentall Discourse.*

When a man thinketh on any thing whatsoever, His next Thought after, is not altogether so casuall as it seems to be. Not every Thought to every Thought succeeds indifferently. But as wee have no Imagination, whereof we have not formerly had Sense, in whole, or in parts; so we have no Transition from one Imagination to another, whereof we never had the like before in our Senses. The reason whereof is this. All Fancies are Motions within us, reliques of those made in the Sense: And those motions that immediately succeeded one another in the sense, continue also together after Sense: In so much as the former comming again to take place, and be prædominant, the later followeth, by coherence of the matter moved, in such manner, as water upon a plain Table is drawn which way any one part of it is guided by the finger. But because in sense, to one and the same thing perceived, sometimes one thing, sometimes another succeedeth, it comes to passe in time, that in the Imagining of any thing, there is no certainty what we shall Imagine next; Onely this is certain, it shall be something that succeeded the same before, at one time or another.

This Trayne of Thoughts, or Mentall Discourse, is of two sorts. The first is *Unguided*, *without Designe*, and inconstant; Wherein there is no Passionate Thought, to govern and direct those that follow, to it self, as the end and scope of some desire, or other passion: In which case the thoughts are said to wander, and seem impertinent one to another, as in a Dream. Such are Commonly the thoughts of men, that are not onely without company, but also without care of any thing; though even then their Thoughts are as busie as at other times, but without harmony; as the sound which a Lute out of tune would yeeld to any man; or in tune, to one that could not play. And yet in this wild ranging of the mind, a man may oft-times perceive the way of it, and the dependance of one thought upon another. For in a Discourse of our present civill warre, what could seem more impertinent, than to ask (as one did) what was the value of a Roman Penny? Yet the Cohærence to me was manifest enough. For the Thought of the warre, introduced the Thought of the delivering up the King to his Enemies; The Thought of that, brought in the Thought of the delivering up of Christ; and that again the Thought of the 30 pence, which was the price of that treason: and thence easily followed that malicious question; and all this in a moment of time; for Thought is quick.

The second is more constant; as being *regulated* by some desire, and designe. For the impression made by such things as wee desire, or feare, is strong, and permanent, or, (if it cease for a time,) of quick return: so strong it is sometimes, as to hinder and break our sleep. From Desire, ariseth the Thought of some means we have seen produce the like of that which we ayme at; and from the thought of that, the thought of means to that mean; and so continually, till we come to some beginning within our own power. And because the End, by the greatnesse of the impression, comes often to mind, in case our thoughts begin to wander, they are quickly again reduced into the way: which observed by one of the seven wise men, made him give men this præcept, which is now worne out, *Respice finem*; that is to say, in all your actions, look often upon what you would have, as the thing that directs all your thoughts in the way to attain it.

The Trayn of regulated Thoughts is of two kinds; One, when of an effect imagined, wee seek the causes, or means that produce it: and this is common to Man and Beast. The other is, when imagining any thing whatsoever, wee seek all the possible effects, that can by it be produced; that is to say, we imagine what we can do with it, when wee have it. Of which I have not at any time seen any signe, but in man onely; for this is a curiosity hardly incident to the nature of any living creature that has no other Passion but sensuall, such as are hunger, thirst, lust, and anger. In summe, the Discourse of the Mind, when it is governed by designe, is nothing but *Seeking*, or the faculty of Invention, which the Latines call *Sagacitas*, and *Solertia*; a hunting out of the causes, of some effect, present or past; or of the effects, of some present or past cause. Sometimes a man seeks what he hath lost; and from that place, and time, wherein hee misses it, his mind runs back, from place to place, and time to time, to find where, and when he had it; that is to say, to find some certain, and limited time and place, in which to begin a method of seeking. Again, from thence, his thoughts run over the same places and times, to find what action, or other occasion might make him lose it. This we call *Remembrance*, or Calling to mind: the Latines call it *Reminiscentia*, as it were a *Re-conning* of our former actions.

Sometimes a man knows a place determinate, within the compasse whereof he is to seek; and then his thoughts run over all the parts thereof, in the same manner, as one would sweep a room, to find a jewell; or as a Spaniel ranges the field, till he find a sent; or as a man should run over the Alphabet, to start a rime.

Sometime a man desires to know the event of an action; and then he thinketh of some like action past, and the events thereof one after another; supposing like events will follow like actions. As he that foresees what wil become of a Criminal, re-cons what he has seen follow on the like Crime before; having this order of thoughts, The Crime, the Officer, the Prison, the Judge, and the Gallowes. Which kind of thoughts, is called *Foresight*, and *Prudence*, or *Providence*; and sometimes *Wisdome*; though such conjecture, through the difficulty of observing all circumstances, be very fallacious. But this is certain; by how much one man has more experience of things past, than another; by so much also he is more Prudent, and his expectations the seldomer faile him. The *Present* onely has a being in Nature; things *Past* have a being in the Memory onely, but things *to come* have no being at all; the *Future* being but a fiction of the mind, applying the sequels of actions Past, to the actions that are Present; which with most certainty is done by him that has most Experience; but not with certainty enough. And though it be called Prudence, when the Event answereth our Expectation; yet in its own nature, it is but Presumption. For the foresight of things to come, which is Providence, belongs onely to him by whose will they are to come. From him onely, and supernaturally, proceeds Prophecy. The best Prophet naturally is the best guesser; and the best guesser, he that is most versed and studied in the matters he guesses at: for he hath most *Signes* to guesse by.

A *Signe*, is the Event Antecedent, of the Consequent; and contrarily, the Consequent of the Antecedent, when the like Consequences have been observed, before: And the oftner they have been observed, the lesse uncertain is the Signe. And therefore he that has most experience in any kind of businesse, has most Signes, whereby to guesse at the Future time; and consequently is the most prudent: And so much more prudent than he that is new in that kind of business, as not to be equalled by any advantage of naturall and extemporary wit: though perhaps many young men think the contrary.

Nevertheless it is not Prudence that distinguisheth man from beast. There be beasts, that at a year old observe more, and pursue that which is for their good, more prudently, than a child can do at ten.

As Prudence is a *Præsumtion* of the *Future*, contracted from the *Experience* of time *Past*: So there is a Præsumtion of things Past taken from other things (not future but) past also. For he that hath seen by what courses and degrees, a flourishing State hath first come into civil warre, and then to ruine; upon the sights of the ruines of any other State, will guesse, the like warre, and the like courses have been there also. But this conjecture, has the same incertainty almost with the conjecture of the Future; both being grounded onely upon Experience.

There is no other act of mans mind, that I can remember, naturally planted in him, so, as to need no other thing, to the exercise of it, but to be born a man, and live with the use of his five Senses. Those other Faculties, of which I shall speak by and by, and which seem proper to man onely, are acquired, and encreased by study and industry; and of most men learned by instruction, and discipline; and proceed all from the invention of Words, and Speech. For besides Sense, and Thoughts, and the Trayne of thoughts, the mind of man has no other motion; though by the help of Speech, and Method, the same Facultyes may be improved to such a height, as to distinguish men from all other living Creatures.

Whatsoever we imagine, is *Finite*. Therefore there is no Idea, or conception of anything we call *Infinite*. No man can have in his mind an Image of infinite magnitude; nor conceive infinite swiftness, infinite time, or infinite force, or infinite power. When we say any thing is infinite, we signifie onely, that we are not able to conceive the ends, and bounds of the thing named; having no Conception of the thing, but of our own inability. And therefore the Name of *God* is used, not to make us conceive him; (for he is *Incomprehensible*; and his greatnesse, and power are unconceivable;) but that we may honour him. Also because whatsoever (as I said before,) we conceive, has been perceived first by sense, either all at once, or by parts; a man can have no thought, representing any thing, not subject to sense. No man therefore can conceive any thing, but he must conceive it in some place; and indued with some determinate magnitude; and which may be divided into parts; nor that any thing is all in this place, and all in another place at the same time; nor that two, or more things can be in one, and the same place at once: For none of these things ever have, or can be incident to Sense; but are absurd speeches, taken upon credit (without any signification at all,) from deceived Philosophers, and deceived, or deceiving Schoolemen.

Of SPEECH

The Invention of *Printing*, though ingenious, compared with the invention of *Letters*, is no great matter. But who was the first that found the use of Letters, is not known. He that first brought them into *Greece*, men say was *Cadmus*, the sonne of *Agenor*, King of Phænicia. A profitable Invention for continuing the memory of time past, and the conjunction of mankind, dispersed into so many, and distant regions of the Earth; and with all difficult, as proceeding from a watchfull observation of the divers motions of the Tongue, Palat, Lips, and other organs of Speech; whereby to make as many differences of characters, to remember them. But the most noble and profitable invention of all other, was that of SPEECH, consisting of *Names* or *Appellations*, and their Connexion; whereby men register their Thoughts; recall them when they are past; and also declare them one to another for mutuall utility and conversation; without which, there had been amongst men, neither Common-wealth, nor Society, nor Contract, nor Peace, no more than amongst Lyons, Bears, and Wolves. The first author of Speech was *God* himself, that instructed *Adam* how to name such creatures as he presented to his sight; For the Scripture goeth no further in this matter. But this was sufficient to direct him to adde more names, as the experience and use of the creatures should give him occasion; and to joyn them in such manner by degrees, as to make himself understood; and so by succession of time, so much language might be gotten, as he had found use for; though not so copious, as an Orator or Philosopher has need of. For I do not find any thing in the Scripture, out of which, directly or by consequence can be gathered, that *Adam* was taught the names of all Figures, Numbers, Measures, Colours, Sounds, Fancies, Relations; much less the names of Words and Speech, as *Generall*, *Speciall*, *Affirmative*, *Negative*, *Interrogative*, *Optative*, *Infinitive*, all which are usefull; and least of all, of *Entity*, *Intentionality*, *Quiddity*, and other insignificant words of the School.

But all this language gotten, and augmented by *Adam* and his posterity, was again lost at the tower of *Babel*, when by the hand of God, every man was stricken for his rebellion, with an oblivion of his former language. And being hereby forced to disperse themselves into severall parts of the world, it must needs be, that the diversity of Tongues that now is, proceeded by degrees from them, in such manner, as need (the mother of all inventions) taught them; and in tract of time grew every where more copious.

The generall use of Speech, is to transferre our Mentall Discourse, into Verbal; or the Trayne of our Thoughts, into a Trayne of Words; and that for two commodities; whereof one is, the Registring of the Consequences of our Thoughts; which being apt to slip out of our memory, and put us to a new labour, may again be recalled, by such words as they were marked by. So that the first use of names, is to serve for *Markes*, or *Notes* of remembrance. Another is, when many use the same words, to signifie (by their connexion and order,) one to another, what they conceive, or think of each matter; and also what they desire, feare, or have any other passion for. And for this use they are called *Signes*. Speciall uses of Speech are these; First, to Register, what by cogitation, wee find to be the cause of any thing, present or past; and what we find things present or past may produce, or effect: which in summe, is acquiring of Arts. Secondly, to shew to others that knowledge which we have attained; which is, to Counsell, and Teach one another. Thirdly, to make known to others our wills, and purposes, that we may have the mutuall help of one another. Fourthly, to please and delight our selves, and others, by playing with our words, for pleasure or ornament, innocently.

To these Uses, there are also foure correspondent Abuses. First, when men register their thoughts wrong, by the inconstancy of the signification of their words; by which they register for their conceptions, that which they never conceived; and so deceive themselves. Secondly, when they use words metaphorically; that is, in other sense than that they are ordained for; and thereby deceive others. Thirdly, when by words they declare that to be their will, which is not. Fourthly, when they use them to grieve one another: for seeing nature hath armed living creatures, some with teeth, some with horns, and some with hands, to grieve an enemy, it is but an abuse of Speech, to grieve him with the tongue, unlesse it be one whom wee are obliged to govern; and then it is not to grieve, but to correct and amend.

The manner how Speech serveth to the remembrance of the consequence of causes and effects, consisteth in the imposing of *Names*, and the *Connexion* of them.

Of Names, some are *Proper*, and singular to one onely thing; as *Peter, John, This man, this Tree*: and some are *Common* to many things; as *Man, Horse, Tree*; every of which though but one Name, is nevertheless the name of divers particular things; in respect of all which together, it is called an *Universall*; there being nothing in the world Universall but Names; for the things named, are every one of them Individuall and Singular.

One Universall name is imposed on many things, for their similitude in some quality, or other accident: And whereas a Proper Name bringeth to mind one thing onely; Universals recall any one of those many.

And of Names Universall, some are of more, and some of lesse extent; the larger comprehending the lesse large: and some again of equall extent, comprehending each other reciprocally. As for example, the Name *Body* is of larger signification than the word *Man*, and comprehend-

eth it; and the names *Man* and *Rationall*, are of equall
extent, comprehending mutually one another. But here
wee must take notice, that by a Name is not always
understood, as in Grammar, one onely Word; but sometimes by circumlocution many words together. For all
these words, *Hee that in his actions observeth the Lawes of
his Country*, make but one Name, equivalent to this one
word, *Just*.

By this imposition of Names, some of larger, some
of stricter signification, we turn the reckoning of the
consequences of things imagined in the mind, into a
reckoning of the consequences of Appellations. For
example, a man that hath no use of Speech at all, (such,
as is born and remains perfectly deafe and dumb,) if he
set before his eyes a triangle, and by it two right angles,
(such as are the corners of a square figure,) he may by
meditation compare and find, that the three angles of
that triangle, are equall to those two right angles that
stand by it. But if another triangle be shewn him different
in shape from the former, he cannot know without a
new labour, whether the three angles of that also be
equall to the same. But he that hath the use of words,
when he observes, that such equality was consequent,
not to the length of the sides, nor to any other particular
thing in his triangle; but onely to this, that the sides were
straight, and the angles three; and that that was all, for
which he named it a Triangle; will boldly conclude
Universally, that such equality of angles is in all triangles
whatsoever; and register his invention in these generall
termes, *Every triangle hath its three angles equall to two
right angles*. And thus the consequence found in one

particular, comes to be registred and remembred, as an Universall rule; and discharges our mentall reckoning, of time and place; and delivers us from all labour of the mind, saving the first; and makes that which was found true *here*, and *now*, to be true in *all times* and *places*.

But the use of words in registring our thoughts, is in nothing so evident as in Numbering. A naturall foole that could never learn by heart the order of numerall words, as *one*, *two*, and *three*, may observe every stroak of the Clock, and nod to it, or say one, one, one; but can never know what houre it strikes. And it seems, there was a time when those names of number were not in use; and men were fayn to apply their fingers of one or both hands, to those things they desired to keep account of; and that thence it proceeded, that now our numerall words are but ten, in any Nation, and in some but five, and then they begin again. And he that can tell ten, if he recite them out of order, will lose himselfe, and not know when he has done: Much lesse will he be able to adde, and substract, and performe all other operations of Arithmetique. So that without words, there is no possibility of reckoning of Numbers; much lesse of Magnitudes, of Swiftnesse, of Force, and other things, the reckonings whereof are necessary to the being, or well-being of man-kind.

When two Names are joyned together into a Consequence, or Affirmation; as thus, *A man is a living creature*; or thus, *if he be a man, he is a living creature*, If the later name *Living creature*, signifie all that the former name *Man* signifieth, then the affirmation, or consequence is *true*; otherwise *false*. For *True* and *False* are attributes of

Speech, not of Things. And where Speech is not, there is neither *Truth* nor *Falshood*. *Errour* there may be, as when wee expect that which shall not be; or suspect what has not been: but in neither case can a man be charged with Untruth.

Seeing then that *truth* consisteth in the right ordering of names in our affirmations, a man that seeketh precise *truth*, had need to remember what every name he uses stands for; and to place it accordingly; or else he will find himselfe entangled in words, as a bird in lime-twiggs; the more he struggles, the more belimed. And therefore in Geometry, (which is the onely Science that it hath pleased God hitherto to bestow on mankind,) men begin at settling the significations of their words; which settling of significations, they call *Definitions*; and place them in the beginning of their reckoning.

By this it appears how necessary it is for any man that aspires to true Knowledge, to examine the Definitions of former Authors; and either to correct them, where they are negligently set down; or to make them himselfe. For the errours of Definitions multiply themselves, according as the reckoning proceeds; and lead men into absurdities, which at last they see, but cannot avoyd, without reckoning anew from the beginning; in which lyes the foundation of their errours. From whence it happens, that they which trust to books, do as they that cast up many little summs into a greater, without considering whether those little summes were rightly cast up or not; and at last finding the errour visible, and not mistrusting their first grounds, know not which way to cleere themselves; but spend time in fluttering over their bookes; as birds that entring by the chimney, and finding themselves inclosed in a chamber, flutter at the false light of a glasse window, for want of wit to consider which way they came in. So that in the right Definition of Names, lyes the first use of Speech; which is the Acquisition of Science: And in wrong, or no Definitions, lyes the first abuse; from which proceed all false and senslesse Tenets; which make those men that take their instruction from the authority of books, and not from their own meditation, to be as much below the condition of ignorant men, as men endued with true Science are above it. For between true Science, and erroneous Doctrines, Ignorance is in the middle. Naturall sense and imagination, are not subject to absurdity. Nature it selfe cannot erre: and as men abound in copiousnesse of language; so they become more wise, or more mad than ordinary. Nor is it possible without Letters for any man to become either excellently wise, or (unless his memory be hurt by disease, or ill constitution of organs) excellently foolish. For words are wise mens counters, they do but reckon by them: but they are the mony of fooles, that value them by the authority of an *Aristotle*, a *Cicero*, or a *Thomas*, or any other Doctor whatsoever, if but a man.

Subject to Names, is whatsoever can enter into, or be considered in an account; and be added one to another to make a summe; or substracted one from another, and leave a remainder. The Latines called Accounts of mony *Rationes*, and accounting, *Ratiocinatio*: and that which we in bills or books of account call *Items*, they called *Nomina*; that is, *Names*: and thence it seems to proceed, that they extended the word *Ratio*, to the faculty of Reckoning in all other things. The Greeks have but one word λόγος, for both *Speech* and *Reason*; not that they thought there was no Speech without Reason; but no Reasoning without Speech: And the act of reasoning they called *Syllogisme*; which signifieth summing up of the consequences of one saying to another. And because the same things may enter into account for divers accidents; their names are (to shew that diversity) diversly wrested, and diversified. This diversity of names may be reduced to foure generall heads.

First, a thing may enter into account for *Matter*, or *Body*; as *living, sensible, rationall, hot, cold, moved, quiet*; with all which names the word *Matter*, or *Body* is understood; all such, being names of Matter.

Secondly, it may enter into account, or be considered, for some accident or quality, which we conceive to be in it; as for *being moved*, for *being so long*, for *being hot*, &c; and then, of the name of the thing it selfe, by a little change or wresting, wee make a name for that accident, which we consider; and for *living* put into account *life*; for *moved, motion*; for *hot, heat*; for *long, length*, and the like? And all such Names, are the names of the accidents and properties, by which one Matter, and Body is distinguished from another. These are called *names Abstract*; because severed (not from Matter, but) from the account of Matter.

Thirdly, we bring into account, the Properties of our own bodies, whereby we make such distinction: as when any thing is *Seen* by us, we reckon not the thing it selfe; but the *sight*, the *Colour*, the *Idea* of it in the fancy: and when any thing is *heard*, wee reckon it not; but the *hearing*, or *sound* onely, which is our fancy or conception of it by the Eare: and such are names of fancies.

Fourthly, we bring into account, consider, and give names, to *Names* themselves, and to *Speeches*: For, *generall*, *universall*, *speciall*, *æquivocall*, are names of Names. And *Affirmation*, *Interrogation*, *Commandement*, *Narration*, *Syllogisme*, *Sermon*, *Oration*, and many other such, are names of Speeches. And this is all the variety of Names *positive*; which are put to mark somewhat which is in Nature, or may be feigned by the mind of man, as Bodies that are, or may be conceived to be; or of bodies, the Properties that are, or may be feigned to be; or Words and Speech.

There be also other Names, called *Negative*; which are notes to signifie that a word is not the name of the thing in question; as these words *Nothing*, *no man*, *infinite*, *indocible*, *three want foure*, and the like; which are nevertheless of use in reckoning, or in correcting of reckoning; and call to mind our past cogitations, though they be not names of any thing; because they make us refuse to admit of Names not rightly used.

All other Names, are but insignificant sounds; and those of two sorts. One, when they are new, and yet their meaning not explained by Definition; whereof there have been aboundance coyned by Schoole-men, and pusled Philosophers.

Another, when men make a name of two Names, whose significations are contradictory and inconsistent; as this name, an *incorporeall body*, or (which is all one) an *incorporeall substance*, and a great number more. For whensoever any affirmation is false, the two names of which it is composed, put together and made one, signifie nothing at all. For example, if it be a false affirmation to say *a quadrangle is round*, the word *round quadrangle* signifies nothing; but is a meere sound. So likewise if it be false, to say that vertue can be powred, or blown up and down; the words *In-powred vertue*, *In-blown vertue*, are as absurd and insignificant, as a *round quadrangle*. And therefore you shall hardly meet with a senselesse and insignificant word, that is not made up of some Latin or Greek names. A Frenchman seldome hears our Saviour called by the name of *Parole*, but by the name of *Verbe* often; yet *Verbe* and *Parole* differ no more, but that one is Latin, the other French.

When a man upon the hearing of any Speech, hath those thoughts which the words of that Speech, and their connexion, were ordained and constituted to signifie; Then he is said to understand it: *Understanding* being nothing else, but conception caused by Speech. And therefore if Speech be peculiar to man (as for ought I know it is,) then is Understanding peculiar to him also. And therefore of absurd and false affirmations, in case they be universall, there can be no Understanding; though many think they understand, then, when they do but repeat the words softly, or con them in their mind.

What kinds of Speeches signifie the Appetites, Aversions, and Passions of mans mind; and of their use and abuse, I shall speak when I have spoken of the Passions.

The names of such things as affect us, that is, which please, and displease us, because all men be not alike affected with the same thing, nor the same man at all times, are in the common discourses of men, of *inconstant* signification. For seeing all names are imposed to signifie our conceptions; and all our affections are but conceptions; when we conceive the same things differently, we can hardly avoyd different naming of them. For though the nature of that we conceive, be the same; yet the diversity of our reception of it, in respect of different constitutions of body, and prejudices of opinion, gives everything a tincture of our different passions. And therefore in reasoning, a man must take heed of words; which besides the signification of what we imagine of their nature, have a signification also of the nature, disposition, and interest of the speaker; such as are the names of Vertues, and Vices; For one man calleth *Wisdome*, what another calleth *feare*; and one *cruelty*, what another *justice*; one *prodigality*, what another *magnanimity*; and one *gravity*, what another *stupidity*, &c. And therefore such names can never be true grounds of any ratiocination. No more can Metaphors, and Tropes of speech: but these are less dangerous, because they profess their inconstancy; which the other do not.

[. . .]

Of the Interiour Beginnings of Voluntary Motions; commonly called the PASSIONS. *And the Speeches by which they are expressed.*

There be in Animals, two sorts of *Motions* peculiar to them: One called *Vitall*; begun in generation, and continued without interruption through their whole life; such as are the *course* of the *Bloud*, the *Pulse*, the *Breathing*, the *Concoction*, *Nutrition*, *Excretion*, &c; to which Motions there needs no help of Imagination: The other is *Animall motion*, otherwise called *Voluntary motion*; as to *go*, to *speak*, to *move* any of our limbes, in such manner as is first fancied in our minds. That Sense, is Motion in the organs and interiour parts of mans body, caused by the action of the things we See, Heare, &c; And that Fancy is but the Reliques of the same Motion, remaining after Sense, has been already sayd in the first and second Chapters. And because *going*, *speaking*, and the like Voluntary motions, depend alwayes upon a precedent thought of *whither*, *which way*, and *what*; it is evident, that the Imagination is the first internall beginning of all Voluntary Motion. And although unstudied men, doe not conceive any motion at all to be there, where the thing moved is invisible; or the space it is moved in, is (for the shortnesse of it) insensible; yet that doth not hinder, but that such Motions are. For let a space be never so little, that which is moved over a greater space, whereof that little one is part, must first be moved over that. These small beginnings of Motion, within the body of Man, before they appear in walking, speaking,

striking, and other visible actions, are commonly called
ENDEAVOUR.

This Endeavour, when it is toward something which
causes it, is called APPETITE, or DESIRE; the later, being
the generall name; and the other, oftentimes restrayned
to signifie the Desire of Food, namely *Hunger* and *Thirst*.
And when the Endeavour is fromward something, it is
generally called AVERSION. These words *Appetite*, and
Aversion we have from the *Latines*; and they both of them
signifie the motions, one of approaching, the other of
retiring. So also do the Greek words for the same, which
are ὁρμὴ, and ἀφορμὴ. For Nature it selfe does often
presse upon men those truths, which afterwards, when
they look for somewhat beyond Nature, they stumble
at. For the Schooles find in meere Appetite to go, or
move, no actuall Motion at all: but because some Motion
they must acknowledge, they call it Metaphoricall
Motion; which is but an absurd speech: for though
Words may be called metaphoricall; Bodies, and Motions
cannot.

That which men Desire, they are also sayd to LOVE:
and to HATE those things, for which they have Aversion.
So that Desire, and Love, are the same thing; save that
by Desire, we alwayes signifie the Absence of the Object;
by Love, most commonly the Presence of the same. So
also by Aversion, we signifie the Absence; and by Hate,
the Presence of the Object.

Of Appetites, and Aversions, some are born with
men; as Appetite of food, Appetite of excretion, and
exoneration, (which may also and more properly be
called Aversions, from somewhat they feele in their

Bodies;) and some other Appetites, not many. The rest, which are Appetites of particular things, proceed from Experience, and triall of their effects upon themselves, or other men. For of things wee know not at all, or believe not to be, we can have no further Desire, than to tast and try. But Aversion wee have for things, not onely which we know have hurt us; but also that we do not know whether they will hurt us, or not.

Those things which we neither Desire, nor Hate, we are said to *Contemne*: CONTEMPT being nothing else but an immobility, or contumacy of the Heart, in resisting the action of certain things; and proceeding from that the Heart is already moved otherwise, by other more potent objects; or from want of experience of them.

And because the constitution of a mans Body, is in continuall mutation; it is impossible that all the same things should alwayes cause in him the same Appetites, and Aversions: much lesse can all men consent, in the Desire of almost any one and the same Object.

But whatsoever is the object of any mans Appetite or Desire; that is it, which he for his part calleth *Good*: And the object of his Hate, and Aversion, *Evill*; And of his Contempt, *Vile*, and *Inconsiderable*. For these words of Good, Evill, and Contemptible, are ever used with relation to the person that useth them: There being nothing simply and absolutely so; nor any common Rule of Good and Evill, to be taken from the nature of the objects themselves; but from the Person of the man (where there is no Common-wealth;) or, (in a Common-wealth,) from the Person that representeth it; or from an Arbitrator or Judge, whom men disagreeing shall by consent set up, and make his sentence the Rule thereof.

The Latine Tongue has two words, whose significations approach to those of Good and Evill; but are not precisely the same; And those are *Pulchrum* and *Turpe*. Whereof the former signifies that, which by some apparent signes promiseth Good; and the later, that, which promiseth Evil. But in our Tongue we have not so generall names to expresse them by. But for *Pulchrum*, we say in some things, *Fayre*; in others *Beautifull*, or *Handsome*, or *Gallant*, or *Honourable*, or *Comely*, or *Amiable*; and for *Turpe*, *Foule*, *Deformed*, *Ugly*, *Base*, *Nauseous*, and the like, as the subject shall require; All which words, in their proper places signifie nothing els, but the *Mine*, or Countenance, that promiseth Good and Evil. So that of Good there be three kinds; Good in the Promise, that is *Pulchrum*; Good in Effect, as the end desired, which is called *Jucundum*, *Delightfull*; and Good as the Means, which is called *Utile*, *Profitable*; and as many of Evil: For *Evill*, in Promise, is that they call *Turpe*; Evil in Effect, and End, is *Molestum*, *Unpleasant*, *Troublesome*; and Evill in the Means, *Inutile*, *Unprofitable*, *Hurtfull*.

As, in Sense, that which is really within us, is (as I have sayd before) onely Motion, caused by the action of externall objects, but in apparence; to the Sight, Light and Colour; to the Eare, Sound; to the Nostrill, Odour, &c: so, when the action of the same object is continued from the Eyes, Eares, and other organs to the Heart; the reall effect there is nothing but Motion, or Endeavour; which consisteth in Appetite, or Aversion, to, or from the object moving. But the apparence, or sense of that motion, is that wee either call DELIGHT, or TROUBLE OF MIND.

This Motion, which is called Appetite, and for the apparence of it *Delight*, and *Pleasure*, seemeth to be, a corroboration of Vitall motion, and a help thereunto; and therefore such things as caused Delight, were not improperly called *Jucunda*, (*à Juvando*,) from helping or fortifying; and the contrary, *Molesta*, *Offensive*, from hindering, and troubling the motion vitall.

Pleasure therefore, (or *Delight*,) is the apparence, or sense of Good; and *Molestation* or *Displeasure*, the apparence, or sense of Evill. And consequently all Appetite, Desire, and Love, is accompanied with some Delight more or lesse; and all Hatred, and Aversion, with more or lesse Displeasure and Offence.

Of Pleasures, or Delights, some arise from the sense of an object Present; And those may be called *Pleasures of Sense*, (The word *sensuall*, as it is used by those onely that condemn them, having no place till there be Lawes.) Of this kind are all Onerations and Exonerations of the body; as also all that is pleasant in the *Sight*, *Hearing*, *Smell*, *Tast*, *or Touch*; Others arise from the Expectation, that proceeds from foresight of the End, or Consequence of things; whether those things in the Sense Please or Displease: And these are *Pleasures of the Mind* of him that draweth those consequences; and are generally called JOY. In the like manner, Displeasures, are some in the Sense, and called PAYNE; others, in the Expectation of consequences, and are called GRIEFE.

These simple Passions called *Appetite*, *Desire*, *Love*, *Aversion*, *Hate*, *Joy*, and *Griefe*, have their names for divers considerations diversified. As first, when they one succeed another, they are diversly called from the opinion men have of the likelihood of attaining what they desire. Secondly, from the object loved or hated. Thirdly, from the consideration of many of them together. Fourthly, from the Alteration or succession it selfe.

For *Appetite* with an opinion of attaining, is called HOPE.

The same, without such opinion, DESPAIRE.

Aversion, with opinion of *Hurt* from the object, FEARE.

The same, with hope of avoyding that Hurt by resistence, COURAGE.

Sudden *Courage*, ANGER.

Constant *Hope*, CONFIDENCE of our selves.

Constant *Despayre*, DIFFIDENCE of our selves.

Anger for great hurt done to another, when we conceive the same to be done by Injury, INDIGNATION.

Desire of good to another, BENEVOLENCE, GOOD WILL, CHARITY. If to man generally, GOOD NATURE.

Desire of Riches, COVETOUSNESSE: a name used alwayes in signification of blame; because men contending for them, are displeased with one anothers attaining them; though the desire in it selfe, be to be blamed, or allowed, according to the means by which those Riches are sought.

Desire of Office, or precedence, AMBITION: a name used also in the worse sense, for the reason before mentioned.

Desire of things that conduce but a little to our ends; And fear of things that are but of little hindrance, PUSILLANIMITY.

Contempt of little helps, and hindrances, MAG-NANIMITY.

Magnanimity, in danger of Death, or Wounds, VAL-OUR, FORTITUDE.

Magnanimity, in the use of Riches, LIBERALITY.

Pusillanimity, in the same WRETCHEDNESSE, MISER-ABLENESSE; or PARSIMONY; as it is liked, or disliked.

Love of Persons for society, KINDNESSE.

Love of Persons for Pleasing the sense onely, NATURAL LUST.

Love of the same, acquired from Rumination, that is, Imagination of Pleasure past, LUXURY.

Love of one singularly, with desire to be singularly beloved, THE PASSION OF LOVE. The same, with fear that the love is not mutuall, JEALOUSIE.

Desire, by doing hurt to another, to make him condemn some fact of his own, REVENGEFULNESSE.

Desire, to know why, and how, CURIOSITY; such as is in no living creature but *Man*; so that Man is distinguished, not onely by his Reason; but also by this singular Passion from other *Animals*; in whom the appetite of food, and other pleasures of Sense, by prædominance, take away the care of knowing causes; which is a Lust of the mind, that by a perseverance of delight in the continuall and indefatigable generation of Knowledge, exceedeth the short vehemence of any carnall Pleasure.

Feare of power invisible, feigned by the mind, or imagined from tales publiquely allowed, RELIGION; not allowed, SUPERSTITION. And when the power imagined, is truly such as we imagine, TRUE RELIGION.

Feare, without the apprehension of why, or what,

PANIQUE TERROR; called so from the Fables, that make *Pan* the author of them; whereas in truth, there is alwayes in him that so feareth, first, some apprehension of the cause, though the rest run away by Example; every one supposing his fellow to know why. And therefore this Passion happens to none but in a throng, or multitude of people.

Joy, from apprehension of novelty, ADMIRATION; proper to Man, because it excites the appetite of knowing the cause.

Joy, arising from imagination of a mans own power and ability, is that exultation of the mind which is called GLORYING: which if grounded upon the experience of his own former actions, is the same with *Confidence*: but if grounded on the flattery of others; or onely supposed by himself, for delight in the consequences of it, is called VAINE-GLORY: which name is properly given; because a well grounded *Confidence* begetteth Attempt; whereas the supposing of power does not, and is therefore rightly called *Vaine*.

Griefe, from opinion of want of power, is called DEJECTION of mind.

The *vain-glory* which consisteth in the feigning or supposing of abilities in our selves, which we know are not, is most incident to young men, and nourished by the Histories, or Fictions of Gallant Persons; and is corrected often times by Age, and Employment.

Sudden Glory, is the passion which maketh those *Grimaces* called LAUGHTER; and is caused either by some sudden act of their own, that pleaseth them; or by the apprehension of some deformed thing in another, by comparison whereof they suddenly applaud themselves. And it is incident most to them, that are conscious of the fewest abilities in themselves; who are forced to keep themselves in their own favour, by observing the imperfections of other men. And therefore much Laughter at the defects of others, is a signe of Pusillanimity. For of great minds, one of the proper workes is, to help and free others from scorn; and compare themselves onely with the most able.

On the contrary, *Sudden Dejection*, is the passion that causeth WEEPING; and is caused by such accidents, as suddenly take away some vehement hope, or some prop of their power: And they are most subject to it, that rely principally on helps externall, such as are Women, and Children. Therefore some Weep for the losse of Friends; Others for their unkindnesse; others for the sudden stop made to their thoughts of revenge, by Reconciliation. But in all cases, both Laughter, and Weeping, are sudden motions; Custome taking them both away. For no man Laughs at old jests; or Weeps for an old calamity.

Griefe, for the discovery of some defect of ability, is SHAME, or the passion that discovereth it selfe in BLUSHING; and consisteth in the apprehension of some thing dishonourable; and in young men, is a signe of the love of good reputation; and commendable: In old men it is a signe of the same; but because it comes too late, not commendable.

The *Contempt* of good Reputation is called IMPUDENCE.

Griefe, for the Calamity of another, is PITTY; and ariseth from the imagination that the like calamity may befall himselfe; and therefore is called also COMPASSION, and in the phrase of this present time a FELLOW-FEELING: And therefore for Calamity arriving from great wickedness, the best men have the least Pitty; and for the same Calamity, those have least Pitty, that think themselves least obnoxious to the same.

Contempt, or little sense of the calamity of others, is that which men call CRUELTY; proceeding from Security of their own fortune. For, that any man should take pleasure in other mens great harmes, without other end of his own, I do not conceive it possible.

Griefe, for the successe of a Competitor in wealth, honour, or other good, if it be joyned with Endeavour to enforce our own abilities to equall or exceed him, is called EMULATION: But joyned with Endeavour to supplant, or hinder a Competitor, ENVIE.

When in the mind of man, Appetites, and Aversions, Hopes, and Feares, concerning one and the same thing, arise alternately; and divers good and evill consequences of the doing, or omitting the thing propounded, come successively into our thoughts; so that sometimes we have an Appetite to it; sometimes an Aversion from it; sometimes Hope to be able to do it; sometimes Despaire, or Feare to attempt it; the whole summe of Desires, Aversions, Hopes and Fears, continued till the thing be either done, or thought impossible, is that we call DELIBERATION.

Therefore of things past, there is no *Deliberation*; because manifestly impossible to be changed: nor of things known to be impossible, or thought so; because men know, or think such Deliberation vain. But of things impossible, which we think possible, we may Deliberate; not knowing it is in vain. And it is called *Deliberation*; because it is a putting an end to the *Liberty* we had of doing, or omitting, according to our own Appetite, or Aversion.

This alternate Succession of Appetites, Aversions, Hopes and Fears, is no lesse in other living Creatures then in Man: and therefore Beasts also Deliberate.

Every *Deliberation* is then sayd to *End*, when that whereof they Deliberate, is either done, or thought impossible; because till then wee retain the liberty of doing, or omitting, according to our Appetite, or Aversion.

In *Deliberation*, the last Appetite, or Aversion, immediately adhæring to the action, or to the omission thereof, is that wee call the WILL; the Act, (not the faculty,) of *Willing*. And Beasts that have *Deliberation*, must necessarily also have *Will*. The Definition of the *Will*, given commonly by the Schooles, that it is a *Rationall Appetite*, is not good. For if it were, then could there be no Voluntary Act against Reason. For a *Voluntary Act* is that, which proceedeth from the *will*, and no other. But if in stead of a Rationall Appetite, we shall say an Appetite resulting from a precedent Deliberation, then the Definition is the same that I have given here. *Will* therefore *is the last Appetite in Deliberating*. And though we say in common Discourse, a man had a Will once to do a thing, that nevertthelesse he forbore to do; yet that is properly but an Inclination, which makes no Action Voluntary; because the action depends not of it, but of the last Inclination, or Appetite. For if the intervenient Appetites, make any action Voluntary; then by the same Reason all intervenient Aversions, should make the same action Involuntary; and so one and the same action, should be both Voluntary & Involuntary.

By this it is manifest, that not onely actions that have their beginning from Covetousnesse, Ambition, Lust, or other Appetites to the thing propounded; but also those that have their beginning from Aversion, or Feare of those consequences that follow the omission, are *voluntary actions*.

The formes of Speech by which the Passions are expressed, are partly the same, and partly different from those, by which wee expresse our Thoughts. And first generally all Passions may be expressed *Indicatively*; as *I love, I feare, I joy, I deliberate, I will, I command:* but some of them have particular expressions by themselves, which neverthelesse are not affirmations, unlesse it be when they serve to make other inferences, besides that of the Passion they proceed from. Deliberation is expressed *Subjunctively*; which is a speech proper to signifie suppositions, with their consequences; as, *If this be done, then this will follow*; and differs not from the language of Reasoning, save that Reasoning is in generall words; but Deliberation for the most part is of Particulars. The language of Desire, and Aversion, is *Imperative*; as *Do this, forbeare that*; which when the party is obliged to do, or forbeare, is *Command*; otherwise *Prayer*; or els *Counsell*. The language of Vain-Glory, of Indignation, Pitty and Revengefulness, *Optative*: But of the Desire to know, there is a peculiar expression, called *Interrogative*; as, *What is it, when shall it, how is it done*, and *why so?* other language of the Passions I find none: For Cursing,

Swearing, Reviling, and the like, do not signifie as Speech; but as the actions of a tongue accustomed.

These formes of Speech, I say, are expressions, or voluntary significations of our Passions: but certain signes they be not; because they may be used arbitrarily, whether they that use them, have such Passions or not. The best signes of Passions present, are either in the countenance, motions of the body, actions, and ends, or aimes, which we otherwise know the man to have.

And because in Deliberation, the Appetites, and Aversions are raised by foresight of the good and evill consequences, and sequels of the action whereof we Deliberate; the good or evill effect thereof dependeth on the foresight of a long chain of consequences, of which very seldome any man is able to see to the end. But for so farre as a man seeth, if the Good in those consequences, be greater than the Evill, the whole chaine is that which Writers call *Apparent*, or *Seeming Good*. And contrarily, when the Evill exceedeth the Good, the whole is *Apparent*, or *Seeming Evill*: so that he who hath by Experience, or Reason, the greatest and surest prospect of Consequences, Deliberates best himself; and is able when he will, to give the best counsell unto others.

Continuall successe in obtaining those things which a man from time to time desireth, that is to say, continuall prospering, is that men call FELICITY; I mean the Felicity of this life. For there is no such thing as perpetuall Tranquillity of mind, while we live here; because Life it selfe is but Motion, and can never be without Desire, nor without Feare, no more than without Sense. What kind of Felicity God hath ordained to them that devoutly honour him, a man shall no sooner know, than enjoy; being joyes, that now are as incomprehensible, as the word of School-men *Beatificall Vision* is unintelligible.

The forme of Speech whereby men signifie their opinion of the Goodnesse of any thing, is PRAISE. That whereby they signifie the power and greatnesse of any thing, is MAGNIFYING. And that whereby they signifie the opinion they have of a mans Felicity, is by the Greeks called μακαρισμός, for which wee have no name in our tongue. And thus much is sufficient for the present purpose, to have been said of the PASSIONS.

[. . .]

Of the NATURALL CONDITION *of Mankind, as concerning their Felicity, and Misery*

Nature hath made men so equall, in the faculties of body, and mind; as that though there bee found one man sometimes manifestly stronger in body, or of quicker mind then another; yet when all is reckoned together, the difference between man, and man, is not so considerable, as that one man can thereupon claim to himselfe any benefit, to which another may not pretend, as well as he. For as to the strength of body, the weakest has strength enough to kill the strongest, either by secret machination, or by confederacy with others, that are in the same danger with himselfe.

And as to the faculties of the mind, (setting aside the arts grounded upon words, and especially that skill of proceeding upon generall, and infallible rules, called Science; which very few have, and but in few things; as being not a native faculty, born with us; nor attained, (as Prudence,) while we look after somewhat els,) I find yet a greater equality amongst men, than that of strength. For Prudence, is but Experience; which equall time, equally bestowes on all men, in those things they equally apply themselves unto. That which may perhaps make such equality incredible, is but a vain conceipt of ones owne wisdome, which almost all men think they have in a greater degree, than the Vulgar; that is, than all men but themselves, and a few others, whom by Fame, or for concurring with themselves, they approve. For such is the nature of men, that howsoever they may acknowledge many others to be more witty, or more eloquent, or more learned; Yet they will hardly believe there be many so wise as themselves: For they see their own wit at hand, and other mens at a distance. But this proveth rather that men are in that point equall, than unequall. For there is not ordinarily a greater signe of the equall distribution of any thing, than that every man is contented with his share.

From this equality of ability, ariseth equality of hope in the attaining of our Ends. And therefore if any two men desire the same thing, which neverthelesse they cannot both enjoy, they become enemies; and in the way to their End, (which is principally their owne conservation, and sometimes their delectation only,) endeavour to destroy, or subdue one an other. And from hence it comes to passe, that where an Invader hath no more to feare, than an other mans single power; if one plant, sow, build, or possesse a convenient Seat, others may probably be expected to come prepared with forces united, to dispossesse, and deprive him, not only of the fruit of his labour, but also of his life, or liberty. And the Invader again is in the like danger of another.

And from this diffidence of one another, there is no way for any man to secure himselfe, so reasonable, as Anticipation; that is, by force, or wiles, to master the persons of all men he can, so long, till he see no other power great enough to endanger him: And this is no more than his own conservation requireth, and is generally allowed. Also because there be some, that taking pleasure in contemplating their own power in the acts of conquest, which they pursue farther than their security requires; if others, that otherwise would be glad to be at ease within modest bounds, should not by invasion increase their power, they would not be able, long time, by standing only on their defence, to subsist. And by consequence, such augmentation of dominion over men, being necessary to a mans conservation, it ought to be allowed him.

Againe, men have no pleasure, (but on the contrary a great deale of griefe) in keeping company, where there is no power able to over-awe them all. For every man looketh that his companion should value him, at the same rate he sets upon himselfe: And upon all signes of contempt, or undervaluing, naturally endeavours, as far as he dares (which amongst them that have no common power, to keep them in quiet, is far enough to make them destroy each other,) to extort a greater value from his contemners, by dommage; and from others, by the example.

So that in the nature of man, we find three principall causes of quarrell. First, Competition; Secondly,
Diffidence; Thirdly, Glory.

The first, maketh men invade for Gain; the second,
for Safety; and the third, for Reputation. The first use
Violence, to make themselves Masters of other mens
persons, wives, children, and cattell; the second, to
defend them; the third, for trifles, as a word, a smile, a
different opinion, and any other signe of undervalue,
either direct in their Persons, or by reflexion in their
Kindred, their Friends, their Nation, their Profession, or
their Name.

Hereby it is manifest, that during the time men live
without a common Power to keep them all in awe, they
are in that condition which is called Warre; and such a
warre, as is of every man, against every man. For
WARRE, consisteth not in Battell onely, or the act of
fighting; but in a tract of time, wherein the Will to
contend by Battell is sufficiently known: and therefore
the notion of *Time*, is to be considered in the nature of
Warre; as it is in the nature of Weather. For as the nature
of Foule weather, lyeth not in a showre or two of rain;
but in an inclination thereto of many dayes together: So
the nature of War, consisteth not in actuall fighting; but
in the known disposition thereto, during all the time
there is no assurance to the contrary. All other time is
PEACE.

Whatsoever therefore is consequent to a time of
Warre, where every man is Enemy to every man; the
same is consequent to the time, wherein men live without other security, than what their own strength, and

their own invention shall furnish them withall. In such condition, there is no place for Industry; because the fruit thereof is uncertain: and consequently no Culture of the Earth; no Navigation, nor use of the commodities that may be imported by Sea; no commodious Building; no Instruments of moving, and removing such things as require much force; no Knowledge of the face of the Earth; no account of Time; no Arts; no Letters; no Society; and which is worst of all, continuall feare, and danger of violent death; And the life of man, solitary, poore, nasty, brutish, and short.

It may seem strange to some man, that has not well weighed these things; that Nature should thus dissociate, and render men apt to invade, and destroy one another: and he may therefore, not trusting to this Inference, made from the Passions, desire perhaps to have the same confirmed by Experience. Let him therefore consider with himselfe, when taking a journey, he armes himselfe, and seeks to go well accompanied; when going to sleep, he locks his dores; when even in his house he locks his chests; and this when he knows there bee Lawes, and publike Officers, armed, to revenge all injuries shall bee done him; what opinion he has of his fellow subjects, when he rides armed; of his fellow Citizens, when he locks his dores; and of his children, and servants, when he locks his chests. Does he not there as much accuse mankind by his actions, as I do by my words? But neither of us accuse mans nature in it. The Desires, and other Passions of man, are in themselves no Sin. No more are the Actions, that proceed from those Passions, till they know a Law that forbids them: which till Lawes be made they cannot know: nor can any Law be made, till they have agreed upon the Person that shall make it.

It may peradventure be thought, there was never such a time, nor condition of warre as this; and I believe it was never generally so, over all the world: but there are many places, where they live so now. For the savage people in many places of *America*, except the government of small Families, the concord whereof dependeth on naturall lust, have no government at all; and live at this day in that brutish manner, as I said before. Howsoever, it may be perceived what manner of life there would be, where there were no common Power to feare; by the manner of life, which men that have formerly lived under a peacefull government, use to degenerate into, in a civill Warre.

But though there had never been any time, wherein particular men were in a condition of warre one against another; yet in all times, Kings, and Persons of Soveraigne authority, because of their Independency, are in continuall jealousies, and in the state and posture of Gladiators; having their weapons pointing, and their eyes fixed on one another; that is, their Forts, Garrisons, and Guns upon the Frontiers of their Kingdomes; and continuall Spyes upon their neighbours; which is a posture of War. But because they uphold thereby, the Industry of their Subjects; there does not follow from it, that misery, which accompanies the Liberty of particular men.

To this warre of every man against every man, this also is consequent; that nothing can be Unjust. The notions of Right and Wrong, Justice and Injustice have there no place. Where there is no common Power, there is no Law: where no Law, no Injustice. Force, and Fraud, are in warre the two Cardinall vertues. Justice, and Injustice are none of the Faculties neither of the Body, nor Mind. If they were, they might be in a man that were alone in the world, as well as his Senses, and Passions. They are Qualities, that relate to men in Society, not in Solitude. It is consequent also to the same condition, that there be no Propriety, no Dominion, no *Mine* and *Thine* distinct; but onely that to be every mans that he can get; and for so long, as he can keep it. And thus much for the ill condition, which man by meer Nature is actually placed in; though with a possiblity to come out of it, consisting partly in the Passions, partly in his Reason.

The Passions that encline men to Peace, are Feare of Death; Desire of such things as are necessary to commodious living; and a Hope by their Industry to obtain them. And Reason suggesteth convenient Articles of Peace, upon which men may be drawn to agreement. These Articles, are they, which otherwise are called the Lawes of Nature: whereof I shall speak more particularly, in the two following Chapters.*

[. . .]

---

* Fourteen and fifteen, not included here.

Of Common-wealth

Of the Causes, Generation, and Definition of a
COMMON-WEALTH

The finall Cause, End, or Designe of men, (who naturally love Liberty, and Dominion over others,) in the introduction of that restraint upon themselves, (in which wee see them live in Common-wealths,) is the foresight of their own preservation, and of a more contented life thereby; that is to say, of getting themselves out from that miserable condition of Warre, which is necessarily consequent (as hath been shewn) to the naturall Passions of men, when there is no visible Power to keep them in awe, and tye them by feare of punishment to the performance of their Covenants, and observation of those Lawes of Nature set down in the fourteenth and fifteenth Chapters.

For the Lawes of Nature (as *Justice*, *Equity*, *Modesty*, *Mercy*, and (in summe) *doing to others, as wee would be done to*,) of themselves, without the terrour of some Power, to cause them to be observed, are contrary to our naturall Passions, that carry us to Partiality, Pride, Revenge, and the like. And Covenants, without the Sword, are but Words, and of no strength to secure a man at all. Therefore notwithstanding the Lawes of Nature, (which every one hath then kept, when he has the will to keep them, when he can do it safely,) if there be no Power erected, or not great enough for our security; every man will and may lawfully rely on his own strength and art, for caution against all other men. And in all places, where men have lived by small Families, to robbe and spoyle one another, has been a Trade, and so farre from being reputed against the Law of Nature, that the greater spoyles they gained, the greater was their honour; and men observed no other Lawes therein, but the Lawes of Honour; that is, to abstain from cruelty, leaving to men their lives, and instruments of husbandry. And as small Familyes did then; so now do Cities and Kingdomes which are but greater Families (for their own security) enlarge their Dominions, upon all pretences of danger, and fear of Invasion, or assistance that may be given to Invaders, endeavour as much as they can, to subdue, or weaken their neighbours, by open force, and secret arts, for want of other Caution, justly; and are remembred for it in after ages with honour.

Nor is it the joyning together of a small number of men, that gives them this security; because in small numbers, small additions on the one side or the other, make the advantage of strength so great, as is sufficient to carry the Victory; and therefore gives encouragement to an Invasion. The Multitude sufficient to confide in for our Security, is not determined by any certain number, but by comparison with the Enemy we feare; and is then sufficient, when the odds of the Enemy is not of so visible and conspicuous moment, to determine the event of warre, as to move him to attempt.

And be there never so great a Multitude; yet if their

actions be directed according to their particular judgements, and particular appetites, they can expect thereby no defence, nor protection, neither against a Common enemy, nor against the injuries of one another. For being distracted in opinions concerning the best use and application of their strength, they do not help, but hinder one another; and reduce their strength by mutuall opposition to nothing: whereby they are easily, not onely subdued by a very few that agree together; but also when there is no common enemy, they make warre upon each other, for their particular interests. For if we could suppose a great Multitude of men to consent in the observation of Justice, and other Lawes of Nature, without a common Power to keep them all in awe; we might as well suppose all Man-kind to do the same; and then there neither would be, nor need to be any Civill Government, or Common-wealth at all; because there would be Peace without subjection.

Nor is it enough for the security, which men desire should last all the time of their life, that they be governed, and directed by one judgement, for a limited time; as in one Battell, or one Warre. For though they obtain a Victory by their unanimous endeavour against a forraign enemy; yet afterwards, when either they have no common enemy, or he that by one part is held for an enemy, is by another part held for a friend, they must needs by the difference of their interests dissolve, and fall again into a Warre amongst themselves.

It is true, that certain living creatures, as Bees, and Ants, live sociably one with another, (which are therefore by *Aristotle* numbred amongst Politicall creatures;) and yet have no other direction, than their particular judgements and appetites; nor speech, whereby one of them can signifie to another, what he thinks expedient for the common benefit: and therefore some man may perhaps desire to know, why Man-kind cannot do the same. To which I answer,

First, that men are continually in competition for Honour and Dignity, which these creatures are not; and consequently amongst men there ariseth on that ground, Envy and Hatred, and finally Warre; but amongst these not so.

Secondly, that amongst these creatures, the Common good differeth not from the Private; and being by nature enclined to their private, they procure thereby the common benefit. But man, whose Joy consisteth in comparing himselfe with other men, can relish nothing but what is eminent.

Thirdly, that these creatures, having not (as man) the use of reason, do not see, nor think they see any fault, in the administration of their common businesse: whereas amongst men, there are very many, that thinke themselves wiser, and abler to govern the Publique, better than the rest; and these strive to reforme and innovate, one this way, another that way; and thereby bring it into Distraction and Civill warre.

Fourthly, that these creatures, though they have some use of voice, in making knowne to one another their desires, and other affections; yet they want that art of words, by which some men can represent to others, that which is Good, in the likenesse of Evill; and Evill, in the likenesse of Good; and augment, or diminish the apparent greatnesse of Good and Evill; discontenting men, and troubling their Peace at their pleasure.

Fiftly, irrationall creatures cannot distinguish be-tweene *Injury*, and *Dammage*; and therefore as long as they be at ease, they are not offended with their fellowes: whereas Man is then most troublesome, when he is most at ease: for then it is that he loves to shew his Wisdome, and controule the Actions of them that governe the Common-wealth.

Lastly, the agreement of these creatures is Naturall; that of men, is by Covenant only, which is Artificiall: and therefore it is no wonder if there be somewhat else required (besides Covenant) to make their Agreement constant and lasting; which is a Common Power, to keep them in awe, and to direct their actions to the Common Benefit.

The only way to erect such a Common Power, as may be able to defend them from the invasion of For-raigners, and the injuries of one another, and thereby to secure them in such sort, as that by their owne industrie, and by the fruites of the Earth, they may nourish them-selves and live contentedly; is, to conferre all their power and strength upon one Man, or upon one Assembly of men, that may reduce all their Wills, by plurality of voices, unto one Will: which is as much as to say, to appoint one man, or Assembly of men, to beare their Person; and every one to owne, and acknowledge him-selfe to be Author of whatsoever he that so beareth their Person, shall Act, or cause to be Acted, in those things which concerne the Common Peace and Safetie; and therein to submit their Wills, every one to his Will, and their Judgements, to his Judgment. This is more than Consent, or Concord; it is a reall Unitie of them all, in one and the same Person, made by Covenant of every man with every man, in such manner, as if every man should say to every man, *I Authorise and give up my Right of Governing my selfe, to this Man, or to this Assembly of men, on this condition, that thou give up thy Right to him, and Authorise all his Actions in like manner.* This done, the Multitude so united in one Person, is called a COMMON-WEALTH, in latine CIVITAS. This is the Generation of that great LEVIATHAN, or rather (to speake more reverently) of that *Mortall God*, to which wee owe under the *Immortall God*, our peace and defence. For by this Authoritie, given him by every particular man in the Common-Wealth, he hath the use of so much Power and Strength conferred on him, that by terror thereof, he is inabled to forme the wills of them all, to Peace at home, and mutuall ayd against their enemies abroad. And in him consisteth the Essence of the Common-wealth; which (to define it,) is *One Person, of whose Acts a great Multitude, by mutuall Covenants one with another, have made themselves every one the Author, to the end he may use the strength and means of them all, as he shall think expedient, for their Peace and Common Defence.*

And he that carryeth this Person, is called SOV-ERAIGNE, and said to have *Soveraigne Power*; and every one besides, his SUBJECT.

The attaining to this Soveraigne Power, is by two wayes. One, by Naturall force; as when a man maketh his children, to submit themselves, and their children to his government, as being able to destroy them if they

refuse; or by Warre subdueth his enemies to his will,
giving them their lives on that condition. The other, is
when men agree amongst themselves, to submit to some
Man, or Assembly of men, voluntarily, on confidence to
be protected by him against all others. This later, may
be called a Politicall Common-wealth or Common-
wealth by *Institution*; and the former, a Common-wealth
by *Acquisition* [. . .]

Of the LIBERTY of Subjects

LIBERTY, or FREEDOME, signifieth (properly) the absence
of Opposition; (by Opposition, I mean externall Impediments of motion;) and may be applyed no lesse to
Irrationall, and Inanimate creatures, than to Rationall.
For whatsoever is so tyed, or environed, as it cannot
move, but within a certain space, which space is determined by the opposition of some externall body, we say
it hath not Liberty to go further. And so of all living
creatures, whilest they are imprisoned, or restrained,
with walls, or chayns; and of the water whilest it is kept
in by banks, or vessels, that otherwise would spread it
selfe into a larger space, we use to say, they are not at
Liberty, to move in such manner, as without those
externall impediments they would. But when the impediment of motion, is in the constitution of the thing it
selfe, we use not to say, it wants the Liberty; but the
Power to move; as when a stone lyeth still, or a man is
fastned to his bed by sicknesse.

And according to this proper, and generally received

meaning of the word, A FREE-MAN, *is he, that in those things, which by his strength and wit he is able to do, is not hindred to doe what he has a will to.* But when the words *Free*, and *Liberty*, are applyed to any thing but *Bodies*, they are abused; for that which is not subject to Motion, is not subject to Impediment: And therefore, when 'tis said (for example) The way is free, no liberty of the way is signified, but of those that walk in it without stop. And when we say a Guift is free, there is not meant any liberty of the Guift, but of the Giver, that was not bound by any law, or Covenant to give it. So when we *speak freely*, it is not the liberty of voice, or pronunciation, but of the man, whom no law hath obliged to speak otherwise then he did. Lastly, from the use of the word *Freewill*, no liberty can be inferred to the will, desire, or inclination, but the liberty of the man; which consisteth in this, that he finds no stop, in doing what he has the will, desire, or inclination to doe.

Feare and Liberty are consistent; as when a man throweth his goods into the Sea for *feare* the ship should sink, he doth it neverthelesse very willingly, and may refuse to doe it if he will: It is therefore the action, of one that was *free*: so a man sometimes pays his debt, only for *feare* of Imprisonment, which because no body hindred him from detaining, was the action of a man at *liberty*. And generally all actions which men doe in Common-wealths, for *feare* of the law, or actions, which the doers had *liberty* to omit.

Liberty and *Necessity* are Consistent: As in the water, that hath not only *liberty*, but a *necessity* of descending by the Channel: so likewise in the Actions which men voluntarily doe; which (because they proceed from their will) proceed from *liberty*; and yet because every act of mans will, and every desire, and inclination proceedeth from some cause, and that from another cause, which causes in a continuall chaine (whose first link in the hand of God the first of all causes) proceed from *necessity*. So that to him that could see the connexion of those causes, the *necessity* of all mens voluntary actions, would appeare manifest. And therefore God, that seeth, and disposeth all things, seeth also that the *liberty* of man in doing what he will, is accompanied with the *necessity* of doing that which God will, & no more, nor lesse. For though men may do many things, which God does not command, nor is therefore Author of them; yet they can have no passion, nor appetite to any thing, of which appetite Gods will is not the cause. And did not his will assure the *necessity* of mans will, and consequently of all that on mans will dependeth, the *liberty* of men would be a contradiction, and impediment to the omnipotence and *liberty* of God. And this shall suffice, (as to the matter in hand) of that naturall *liberty*, which only is properly called *liberty*.

But as men, for the atteyning of peace, and conservation of themselves thereby, have made an Artificiall Man, which we call a Common-wealth; so also have they made Artificiall Chains, called *Civill Lawes*, which they themselves, by mutuall covenants, have fastned at one end, to the lips of that Man, or Assembly, to whom they have given the Soveraigne Power; and at the other end to their own Ears. These Bonds in their own nature but weak, may neverthelesse be made to hold, by the danger, though not by the difficulty of breaking them.

In relation to these Bonds only it is, that I am to speak now, of the *Liberty* of *Subjects*. For seeing there is no Common-wealth in the world, wherein there be Rules enough set down, for the regulating of all the actions, and words of men, (as being a thing impossible:) it followeth necessarily, that in all kinds of actions, by the laws prætermitted, men have the Liberty, of doing what their own reasons shall suggest, for the most profitable to themselves. For if wee take Liberty in the proper sense, for corporall Liberty; that is to say, freedome from chains, and prison, it were very absurd for men to clamor as they doe, for the Liberty they so manifestly enjoy. Againe, if we take Liberty, for an exemption from Lawes, it is no lesse absurd, for men to demand as they doe, that Liberty, by which all other men may be masters of their lives. And yet as absurd as it is, this is it they demand; not knowing that the Lawes are of no power to protect them, without a Sword in the hands of a man, or men, to cause those laws to be put in execution. The Liberty of a Subject, lyeth therefore only in those things, which in regulating their actions, the Soveraign hath prætermitted: such as is the Liberty to buy, and sell, and otherwise contract with one another; to choose their own aboad, their own diet, their own trade of life, and institute their children as they themselves think fit; & the like.

Neverthelesse we are not to understand, that by such Liberty, the Soveraign Power of life, and death, is either abolished, or limited. For it has been already shewn, that nothing the Soveraign Representative can doe to a Subject, on what pretence soever, can properly be called

Injustice, or Injury; because every Subject is Author of
every act the Soveraign doth; so that he never wanteth
Right to any thing, otherwise, than as he himself is the
Subject of God, and bound thereby to observe the laws
of Nature. And therefore it may, and doth often happen
in Common-wealths, that a Subject may be put to death,
by the command of the Soveraign Power; and yet neither
doe the other wrong: As when *Jeptha* caused his daughter
to be sacrificed: In which, and the like cases, he that so
dieth, had Liberty to doe the action, for which he is
neverthelesse, without Injury put to death. And the same
holdeth also in a Soveraign Prince, that putteth to death
an Innocent Subject. For though the action be against
the law of Nature, as being contrary to Equitie, (as was
the killing of *Uriah*, by *David*;) yet it was not an Injurie
to *Uriah*; but to *God*. Not to *Uriah*, because the right to
doe what he pleased, was given him by *Uriah* himself:
And yet to *God*, because *David* was *Gods* Subject; and
prohibited all Iniquitie by the law of Nature. Which
distinction, *David* himself, when he repented the fact,
evidently confirmed, saying, *To thee only have I sinned*.
In the same manner, the people of *Athens*, when they
banished the most potent of their Common-wealth for
ten years, thought they committed no Injustice; and yet
they never questioned what crime he had done; but
what hurt he would doe: Nay they commanded the
banishment of they knew not whom; and every Citizen
bringing his Oystershell into the market place, written
with the name of him he desired should be banished,
without actuall accusing him, sometimes banished an
Aristides, for his reputation of Justice; And sometimes a

scurrilous Jester, as *Hyperbolus*, to make a Jest of it. And yet a man cannot say, the Soveraign People of *Athens* wanted right to banish them; or an *Athenian* the Libertie to Jest, or to be Just.

The Libertie, whereof there is so frequent, and honourable mention, in the Histories, and Philosophy of the Antient Greeks, and Romans, and in the writings, and discourse of those that from them have received all their learning in the Politiques, is not the Libertie of Particular men; but the Libertie of the Common-wealth: which is the same with that, which every man then should have, if there were no Civil Laws, nor Common-wealth at all. And the effects of it also be the same. For as amongst masterlesse men, there is perpetuall war, of every man against his neighbour; no inheritance, to transmit to the Son, nor to expect from the Father; no propriety of Goods, or Lands; no security; but a full and absolute Libertie in every Particular man: So in States, and Common-wealths not dependent on one another, every Common-wealth, (not every man) has an absolute Libertie, to doe what it shall judge (that is to say, what that Man, or Assemblie that representeth it, shall judge) most conducing to their benefit. But withall, they live in the condition of a perpetuall war, and upon the confines of battel, with their frontiers armed, and canons planted against their neighbours round about. The *Athenians*, and *Romanes* were free; that is, free Common-wealths: not that any particular men had the Libertie to resist their own Representative; but that their Representative had the Libertie to resist, or invade other people. There is written on the Turrets of the city of *Luca* in great characters at this day, the word *LIBERTAS*; yet no man can thence inferre, that a particular man has more Libertie, or Immunitie from the service of the Common-wealth there, than in *Constantinople*. Whether a Common-wealth be Monarchicall, or Popular, the Freedome is still the same.

But it is an easy thing, for men to be deceived, by the specious name of Libertie; and for want of Judgement to distinguish, mistake that for their Private Inheritance, and Birth right, which is the right of the Publique only. And when the same errour is confirmed by the authority of men in reputation for their writings in this subject, it is no wonder if it produce sedition, and change of Government. In these westerne parts of the world, we are made to receive our opinions concerning the Institution, and Rights of Common-wealths, from *Aristotle*, *Cicero*, and other men, Greeks and Romanes, that living under Popular States, derived those Rights, not from the Principles of Nature, but transcribed them into their books, out of the Practice of their own Common-wealths, which were Popular; as the Grammarians describe the Rules of Language, out of the Practise of the time; or the Rules of Poetry, out of the Poems of *Homer* and *Virgil*. And because the Athenians were taught, (to keep them from desire of changing their Government,) that they were Freemen, and all that lived under Monarchy were slaves; therefore *Aristotle* puts it down in his *Politiques*, (*lib.6.cap.*2) *In democracy, Liberty is to be supposed: for 'tis commonly held, that no man is Free in any other Government.* And as *Aristotle*; so *Cicero*, and other Writers have grounded their Civil doctrine, on

the opinions of the Romans, who were taught to hate
Monarchy, at first, by them that having deposed their
Soveraign, shared amongst them the Soveraignty of
Rome; and afterwards by their Successors. And by reading
of these Greek, and Latine Authors, men from their
childhood have gotten a habit (under a false shew of
Liberty,) of favouring tumults, and of licentious control-
ling the actions of their Soveraigns; and again of control-
ling those controllers, with the effusion of so much
blood; as I think I may truly say, there was never any
thing so deerly bought, as these Western parts have
bought the learning of the Greek and Latine tongues.

To come now to the particulars of the true Liberty of
a Subject; that is to say, what are the things, which
though commanded by the Soveraign, he may neverthelesse, without Injustice, refuse to do; we are to consider, what Rights we passe away, when we make a
Common-wealth; or (which is all one,) what Liberty we
deny our selves, by owning all the Actions (without
exception) of the Man, or Assembly we make our Soveraign. For in the act of our *Submission*, consisteth both
our *Obligation*, and our *Liberty*; which must therefore be
inferred by arguments taken from thence; there being
no Obligation on any man, which ariseth not from some
Act of his own; for all men equally, are by Nature Free.
And because such arguments, must either be drawn from
the expresse words, *I Authorise all his Actions*, or from the
Intention of him that submitteth himselfe to his Power,
(which Intention is to be understood by the End for
which he so submitteth;) The Obligation, and Liberty of
the Subject, is to be derived, either from those Words,

(or others equivalent;) or else from the End of the Institution of Soveraignty; namely, the Peace of the Subjects within themselves, and their Defence against a common Enemy.

First therefore, seeing Soveraignty by Institution, is by Covenant of every one to every one; and Soveraignty by Acquisition, by Covenants of the Vanquished to the Victor, or Child to the Parent; It is manifest, that every Subject has Liberty in all those things, the right whereof cannot by Covenant be transferred. I have shewn before in the 14. Chapter, that Covenants, not to defend a mans own body, are voyd. Therefore,

If the Soveraign command a man (though justly condemned,) to kill, wound, or mayme himselfe; or not to resist those that assault him; or to abstain from the use of food, ayre, medicine, or any other thing, without which he cannot live; yet hath that man the Liberty to disobey.

If a man be interrogated by the Soveraign, or his Authority, concerning a crime done by himselfe, he is not bound (without assurance of Pardon) to confesse it; because no man (as I have shewn in the same Chapter) can be obliged by Covenant to accuse himselfe.

Again, the Consent of a Subject to Soveraign Power, is contained in these words, *I Authorise, or take upon me, all his actions*; in which there is no restriction at all, of his own former naturall Liberty: For by allowing him to *kill me*, I am not bound to kill my selfe when he commands me. 'Tis one thing to say, *Kill me, or my fellow, if you please*; another thing to say, *I will kill my selfe, or my fellow*. It followeth therefore, that

No man is bound by the words themselves, either to kill himselfe, or any other man; And consequently, that the Obligation a man may sometimes have, upon the Command of the Soveraign to execute any dangerous, or dishonourable Office, dependeth not on the Words of our Submission; but on the Intention; which is to be understood by the End thereof. When therefore our refusall to obey, frustrates the End for which the Soveraignty was ordained; then there is no Liberty to refuse: otherwise there is.

Upon this ground, a man that is commanded as a Souldier to fight against the enemy, though his Soveraign have Right enough to punish his refusall with death, may neverthelesse in many cases refuse, without Injustice; as when he substituteth a sufficient Souldier in his place: for in this case he deserteth not the service of the Common-wealth. And there is allowance to be made for naturall timorousnesse, not onely to women, (of whom no such dangerous duty is expected,) but also to men of feminine courage. When Armies fight, there is on one side, or both, a running away; yet when they do it not out of trechery, but fear, they are not esteemed to do it unjustly, but dishonourably. For the same reason, to avoyd battell, is not Injustice, but Cowardise. But he that inrowleth himselfe a Souldier, or taketh imprest mony, taketh away the excuse of a timorous nature; and is obliged, not onely to go to the battell, but also not to run from it, without his Captaines leave. And when the Defence of the Common-wealth, requireth at once the help of all that are able to bear Arms, every one is obliged; because otherwise the Institution of the

Common-wealth, which they have not the purpose, or courage to preserve, was in vain.

To resist the Sword of the Common-wealth, in defence of another man, guilty, or innocent, no man hath Liberty; because such Liberty, takes away from the Soveraign, the means of Protecting us; and is therefore destructive of the very essence of Government. But in case a great many men together, have already resisted the Soveraign Power unjustly, or committed some Capitall crime, for which every one of them expecteth death, whether have they not the Liberty then to joyn together, and assist, and defend one another? Certainly they have: For they but defend their lives, which the Guilty man may as well do, as the Innocent. There was indeed injustice in the first breach of their duty; Their bearing of Arms subsequent to it, though it be to maintain what they have done, is no new unjust act. And if it be onely to defend their persons, it is not unjust at all. But the offer of Pardon taketh from them, to whom it is offered, the plea of self-defence, and maketh their perseverance in assisting, or defending the rest, unlawfull.

As for other Lyberties, they depend on the silence of the Law. In cases where the Soveraign has prescribed no rule, there the Subject hath the liberty to do, or forbeare, according to his own discretion. And therefore such Liberty is in some places more, and in some lesse; and in some times more, in other times lesse, according as they that have the Soveraignty shall think most convenient. As for Example, there was a time, when in *England* a man might enter in to his own Land, (and dispossesse such as wrongfully possessed it) by force. But in after-times, that Liberty of Forcible entry, was taken away by a Statute made (by the King) in Parliament. And in some places of the world, men have the Liberty of many wives: in other places, such Liberty is not allowed.

If a Subject have a controversie with his Soveraigne, of Debt, or of right of possession of lands or goods, or concerning any service required at his hands, or concerning any penalty corporall, or pecuniary, grounded on a precedent Law; He hath the same Liberty to sue for his right, as if it were against a Subject; and before such Judges, as are appointed by the Soveraign. For seeing the Soveraign demandeth by force of a former Law, and not by vertue of his Power; he declareth thereby, that he requireth no more, than shall appear to be due by that Law. The sute therefore is not contrary to the will of the Soveraign; and consequently the Subject hath the Liberty to demand the hearing of his Cause; and sentence, according to that Law. But if he demand, or take any thing by pretence of his Power; there lyeth, in that case, no action of Law: for all that is done by him in Vertue of his Power, is done by the Authority of every subject, and consequently, he that brings an action against the Soveraign, brings it against himselfe.

If a Monarch, or Soveraign Assembly, grant a Liberty to all, or any of his Subjects; which Grant standing, he is disabled to provide for their safety, the Grant is voyd; unlesse he directly renounce, or transferre the Soveraignty to another. For in that he might openly, (if it had been his will,) and in plain termes, have renounced, or transferred it, and did not; it is to be understood it was not his will; but that the Grant proceeded from

ignorance of the repugnancy between such a Liberty and
the Soveraign Power; and therefore the Soveraignty is
still retayned; and consequently all those Powers, which
are necessary to the exercising thereof; such as are the
Power of Warre, and Peace, of Judicature, of appointing
Officers, and Councellours, of levying Mony, and the
rest named in the 18th Chapter.*

The Obligation of Subjects to the Soveraign, is understood to last as long, and no longer, than the power
lasteth, by which he is able to protect them. For the right
men have by Nature to protect themselves, when none
else can protect them, can by no Covenant be relin-
quished. The Soveraignty is the Soule of the Common-
wealth; which once departed from the Body, the
members doe no more receive their motion from it. The
end of Obedience is Protection; which, wheresoever a
man seeth it, either in his own, or in anothers sword,
Nature applyeth his obedience to it, and his endeavour
to maintaine it. And though Soveraignty, in the intention
of them that make it, be immortall; yet is it in its own
nature, not only subject to violent death, by forreign
war; but also through the ignorance, and passions of
men, it hath in it, from the very institution, many seeds
of a naturall mortality, by Intestine Discord.

If a Subject be taken prisoner in war; or his person, or
his means of life be within the Guards of the enemy,
and hath his life and corporall Libertie given him, on
condition to be Subject to the Victor, he hath Libertie to

---

* Not included here.

accept the condition; and having accepted it, is the subject of him that took him; because he had no other way to preserve himselfe. The case is the same, if he be deteined on the same termes, in a forreign country. But if a man be held in prison, or bonds, or is not trusted with the libertie of his bodie; he cannot be understood to be bound by Covenant to subjection; and therefore may, if he can, make his escape by any means whatsoever.

If a Monarch shall relinquish the Soveraignty, both for himself, and his heires; His Subjects returne to the absolute Libertie of Nature; because, though Nature may declare who are his Sons, and who are the nerest of his Kin; yet it dependeth on his own will, (as hath been said in the precedent chapter,) who shall be his Heyr. If therefore he will have no Heyre, there is no Soveraignty, nor Subjection. The case is the same, if he dye without known Kindred, and without declaration of his Heyre. For then there can no Heire be known, and consequently no Subjection be due.

If the Soveraign Banish his Subject; during the Banishment, he is not Subject. But he that is sent on a message, or hath leave to travell, is still Subject; but it is, by Contract between Soveraigns, not by vertue of the covenant of Subjection. For whosoever entreth into anothers dominion, is Subject to all the Lawes thereof; unlesse he have a privilege by the amity of the Soveraigns, or by speciall licence.

If a Monarch subdued by war, render himself Subject to the Victor; his Subjects are delivered from their former obligation, and become obliged to the Victor. But if he be held prisoner, or have not the liberty of his own Body;

he is not understood to have given away the Right of Soveraigntie; and therefore his Subjects are obliged to yield obedience to the Magistrates formerly placed, governing not in their own name, but in his. For, his Right remaining, the question is only of the Administration; that is to say, of the Magistrates and Officers; which, if he have not means to name, he is supposed to approve those, which he himself had formerly appointed.

[. . .]

Of those things that Weaken, or tend to the DISSOLUTION *of a Common-wealth*

Though nothing can be immortall, which mortals make; yet, if men had the use of reason they pretend to, their Common-wealths might be secured, at least, from perishing by internall diseases. For by the nature of their Institution, they are designed to live, as long as Man-kind, or as the Lawes of Nature, or as Justice it selfe, which gives them life. Therefore when they come to be dissolved, not by externall violence, but intestine disorder, the fault is not in men, as they are the *Matter*; but as they are the *Makers*, and orderers of them. For men, as they become at last weary of irregular justling, and hewing one another, and desire with all their hearts, to conforme themselves into one firme and lasting edifice; so for want, both of the art of making fit Lawes, to square their actions by, and also of humility, and patience, to suffer the rude and combersome points of their present

greatnesse to be taken off, they cannot without the help
of a very able Architect, be compiled, into any other
than a crasie building, such as hardly lasting out their
own time, must assuredly fall upon the heads of their
posterity.

Amongst the *Infirmities* therefore of a Common-
wealth, I will reckon in the first place, those that arise
from an Imperfect Institution, and resemble the diseases
of a naturall body, which proceed from a Defectuous
Procreation.

Of which, this is one, *That a man to obtain a Kingdome,
is sometimes content with lesse Power, than to the Peace, and
defence of the Common-wealth is necessarily required.* From
whence it commeth to passe, that when the exercise of
the Power layd by, is for the publique safety to be
resumed, it hath the resemblance of an unjust act; which
disposeth great numbers of men (when occasion is presented) to rebell; In the same manner as the bodies of
children, gotten by diseased parents, are subject either
to untimely death, or to purge the ill quality, derived
from their vicious conception, by breaking out into biles
and scabbs. And when Kings deny themselves some such
necessary Power, it is not alwayes (though sometimes)
out of ignorance of what is necessary to the office they
undertake; but many times out of a hope to recover the
same again at their pleasure: Wherein they reason not
well; because such as will hold them to their promises,
shall be maintained against them by forraign Common-
wealths; who in order to the good of their own Subjects
let slip few occasions to *weaken* the estate of their Neighbours. So was *Thomas Becket* Archbishop of *Canterbury,*

supported against *Henry* the Second, by the Pope; the subjection of Ecclesiastiques to the Common-wealth, having been dispensed with by *William the Conquerour* at his reception, when he took an Oath, not to infringe the liberty of the Church. And so were the *Barons*, whose power was by *William Rufus* (to have their help in transferring the Succession from his Elder brother, to himselfe,) encreased to a degree, inconsistent with the Soveraign Power, maintained in their Rebellion against King *John*, by the French.

Nor does this happen in Monarchy onely. For whereas the stile of the antient Roman Common-wealth, was, *The Senate, and People of Rome*; neither Senate, nor People pretended to the whole Power; which first caused the seditions, of *Tiberius Gracchus*, *Caius Gracchus*, *Lucius Saturninus*, and others; and afterwards the warres between the Senate and the People, under *Marius* and *Sylla*; and again under *Pompey* and *Cæsar*, to the Extinction of their Democraty, and the setting up of Monarchy.

The people of *Athens* bound themselves but from one onely Action; which was, that no man on pain of death should propound the renewing of the warre for the Island of *Salamis*; And yet thereby, if *Solon* had not caused to be given out he was mad, and afterwards in gesture and habit of a mad-man, and in verse, propounded it to the People that flocked about him, they had had an enemy perpetually in readinesse, even at the gates of their Citie; such dammage, or shifts, are all Common-wealths forced to, that have their Power never so little limited.

In the second place, I observe the *Diseases* of a

Common-wealth, that proceed from the poyson of seditious doctrines; whereof one is, *That every private man is Judge of Good and Evill actions*. This is true in the condition of meer Nature, where there are no Civill Lawes; and also under Civill Government, in such cases as are not determined by the Law. But otherwise, it is manifest, that the measure of Good and Evill actions, is the Civill Law; and the Judge the Legislator, who is alwayes Representative of the Common-wealth. From this false doctrine, men are disposed to debate with themselves, and dispute the commands of the Common-wealth; and afterwards to obey, or disobey them, as in their private judgements they shall think fit. Whereby the Common-wealth is distracted and *Weakened*.

Another doctrine repugnant to Civill Society, is, that *whatsoever a man does against his Conscience, is Sinne*; and it dependeth on the presumption of making himself judge of Good and Evill. For a mans Conscience, and his Judgement is the same thing; and as the Judgement, so also the Conscience may be erroneous. Therefore, though he that is subject to no Civill Law, sinneth in all he does against his Conscience, because he has no other rule to follow but his own reason; yet it is not so with him that lives in a Common-wealth; because the Law is the publique Conscience, by which he hath already undertaken to be guided. Otherwise in such diversity, as there is of private Consciences, which are but private opinions, the Common-wealth must needs be distracted, and no man dare to obey the Soveraign Power, farther than it shall seem good in his own eyes.

It hath been also commonly taught, *That Faith and*

Sanctity, are not to be attained by Study and Reason, but by supernaturall Inspiration, or Infusion, which granted, I see not why any man should render a reason of his Faith; or why every Christian should not be also a Prophet; or why any man should take the Law of his Country, rather than his own Inspiration, for the rule of his action. And thus wee fall again into the fault of taking upon us to Judge of Good and Evill; or to make Judges of it, such private men as pretend to be supernaturally Inspired, to the Dissolution of all Civill Government. Faith comes by hearing, and hearing by those accidents, which guide us into the presence of them that speak to us; which accidents are all contrived by God Almighty; and yet are not supernaturall, but onely, for the great number of them that concurre to every effect, unobservable. Faith, and Sanctity, are indeed not very frequent; but yet they are not Miracles, but brought to passe by education, discipline, correction, and other naturall wayes, by which God worketh them in his elect, at such time as he thinketh fit. And these three opinions, pernicious to Peace and Government, have in this part of the world, proceeded chiefly from the tongues, and pens of un-learned Divines; who joyning the words of Holy Scripture together, otherwise than is agreeable to reason, do what they can, to make men think, that Sanctity and Naturall Reason, cannot stand together.

A fourth opinion, repugnant to the nature of a Common-wealth, is this, *That he that hath the Soveraign Power, is subject to the Civill Lawes*. It is true, that Soveraigns are all subjects to the Lawes of Nature; because such lawes be Divine, and cannot by any man, or

Common-wealth be abrogated. But to those Lawes which the Soveraign himselfe, that is, which the Common-wealth maketh, he is not subject. For to be subject to Lawes, is to be subject to the Common-wealth, that is to the Soveraign Representative, that is to himselfe, which is not subjection, but freedome from the Lawes. Which errour, because it setteth the Lawes above the Soveraign, setteth also a Judge above him, and a Power to punish him; which is to make a new Soveraign; and again for the same reason a third, to punish the second; and so continually without end, to the Confusion, and Dissolution of the Common-wealth.

A Fifth doctrine, that tendeth to the Dissolution of a Common-wealth, is, *That every private man has an absolute Propriety in his Goods; such, as excludeth the Right of the Soveraign*. Every man has indeed a Propriety that excludes the Right of every other Subject: And he has it onely from the Soveraign Power; without the protection whereof, every other man should have equall Right to the same. But if the Right of the Soveraign also be excluded, he cannot performe the office they have put him into; which is, to defend them both from forraign enemies, and from the injuries of one another; and consequently there is no longer a Common-wealth.

And if the Propriety of Subjects, exclude not the Right of the Soveraign Representative to their Goods; much lesse to their offices of Judicature, or Execution, in which they Represent the Soveraign himselfe.

There is a Sixth doctrine, plainly, and directly against the essence of a Common-wealth; and 'tis this, *That the Soveraign Power may be divided*. For what is it to divide the Power of a Common-wealth, but to Dissolve it; for Powers divided mutually destroy each other. And for these doctrines, men are chiefly beholding to some of those, that making profession of the Lawes, endeavour to make them depend upon their own learning, and not upon the Legislative Power.

And as False Doctrine, so also often-times the Example of different Government in a neighbouring Nation, disposeth men to alteration of the forme already setled. So the people of the Jewes were stirred up to reject God, and to call upon the Prophet *Samuel*, for a King after the manner of the Nations: So also the lesser Cities of *Greece*, were continually disturbed, with seditions of the Aristocraticall, and Democraticall factions; one part of almost every Common-wealth, desiring to imitate the Lacedæmonians, the other, the Athenians. And I doubt not, but many men, have been contented to see the late troubles in *England*, out of an imitation of the Low Countries; supposing there needed no more to grow rich, than to change, as they had done, the forme of their Government. For the constitution of mans nature, is of it selfe subject to desire novelty: When therefore they are provoked to the same, by the neighbourhood also of those that have been enriched by it, it is almost impossible for them, not to be content with those that solicite them to change; and love the first beginnings, though they be grieved with the continuance of disorder; like hot blouds, that having gotten the itch, tear themselves with their own nayles, till they can endure the smart no longer.

And as to Rebellion in particular against Monarchy; one of the most frequent causes of it, is the Reading of

the books of Policy, and Histories of the antient Greeks,
and Romans; from which, young men, and all others
that are unprovided of the Antidote of solid Reason,
receiving a strong, and delightfull impression, of the
great exploits of warre, atchieved by the Conductors of
their Armies, receive withall a pleasing Idea, of all they
have done besides; and imagine their great prosperity,
not to have proceeded from the æmulation of particular
men, but from the vertue of their popular forme of
government: Not considering the frequent Seditions, and
Civill warres, produced by the imperfection of their
Policy. From the reading, I say, of such books, men have
undertaken to kill their Kings, because the Greek and
Latine writers, in their books, and discourses of Policy,
make it lawfull, and laudable, for any man so to do;
provided before he do it, he call him Tyrant. For they
say not *Regicide*, that is, killing of a King, but *Tyrannicide*,
that is, killing of a Tyrant is lawfull. From the same
books, they that live under a Monarch conceive an
opinion, that the Subjects in a Popular Common-wealth
enjoy Liberty; but that in a Monarchy they are all Slaves.
I say, they that live under a Monarchy conceive such an
opinion; not they that live under a Popular Government:
for they find no such matter. In summe, I cannot imagine,
how anything can be more prejudiciall to a Monarchy,
than the allowing of such books to be publikely read,
without present applying such correctives of discreet
Masters, as are fit to take away their Venime: Which
Venime I will not doubt to compare to the biting of
a mad Dogge, which is a disease the Physicians call
Hydrophobia, or *fear of Water*. For as he that is so bitten,

has a continuall torment of thirst, and yet abhorreth water; and is in such an estate, as if the poyson endeavoured to convert him into a Dogge: So when a Monarchy is once bitten to the quick, by those Democraticall writers, that continually snarle at that estate; it wanteth nothing more than a strong Monarch, which neverthelesse out of a certain *Tyrannophobia*, or feare of being strongly governed, when they have him, they abhorre.

As there have been Doctors, that hold there be three Soules in a man; so there be also that think there may be more Soules, (that is, more Soveraigns,) than one, in a Common-wealth; and set up a *Supremacy* against the *Soveraignty*; *Canons* against *Lawes*; and a *Ghostly Authority* against the *Civill*; working on mens minds, with words and distinctions, that of themselves signifie nothing, but bewray (by their obscurity) that there walketh (as some think invisibly) another Kingdome, as it were a Kingdome of Fayries, in the dark. Now seeing it is manifest, that the Civill Power, and the Power of the Commonwealth is the same thing; and that Supremacy, and the Power of making Canons, and granting Faculties, implyeth a Common-wealth; it followeth, that where one is Soveraign, another Supreme; where one can make Lawes, and another make Canons; there must needs be two Common-wealths, of one & the same Subjects; which is a Kingdome divided in it selfe, and cannot stand. For notwithstanding the insignificant distinction of *Temporall*, and *Ghostly*, they are still two Kingdomes, and every Subject is subject to two Masters. For seeing the *Ghostly* Power challengeth the Right to declare what is Sinne it challengeth by consequence to declare what is Law, (Sinne being nothing but the transgression of the Law;) and again, the Civill Power challenging to declare what is Law, every Subject must obey two Masters, who both will have their Commands be observed as Law; which is impossible. Or, if it be but one Kingdome, either the *Civill*, which is the Power of the Common-wealth, must be subordinate to the *Ghostly*, and then there is no Soveraignty but the *Ghostly*; or the *Ghostly* must be subordinate to the *Temporall* and then there is no *Supremacy* but the *Temporall*. When therefore these two Powers oppose one another, the Common-wealth cannot but be in great danger of Civill warre, and Dissolution. For the *Civill* Authority being more visible, and standing in the cleerer light of naturall reason cannot choose but draw to it in all times a very considerable part of the people: And the *Spirituall*, though it stand in the darknesse of Schoole distinctions, and hard words; yet because the fear of Darknesse, and Ghosts, is greater than other fears, cannot want a party sufficient to Trouble, and sometimes to Destroy a Common-wealth. And this is a Disease which not unfitly may be compared to the Epilepsie, or Falling-sicknesse (which the Jewes took to be one kind of possession by Spirits) in the Body Naturall. For as in this Disease, there is an unnaturall spirit, or wind in the head that obstructeth the roots of the Nerves, and moving them violently, taketh away the motion which naturally they should have from the power of the Soule in the Brain, and thereby causeth violent, and irregular motions (which men call Convulsions) in the parts; insomuch as he that is seized therewith, falleth down sometimes into the water, and sometimes into the fire, as a man deprived of his senses; so also in the Body Politique, when the Spirituall power, moveth the Members of a Common-wealth, by the terrour of punishments, and hope of rewards (which are the Nerves of it,) otherwise than by the Civill Power (which is the Soule of the Common-wealth) they ought to be moved; and by strange, and hard words suffocates their understanding, it must needs thereby Distract the people, and either Overwhelm the Common-wealth with Oppression, or cast it into the Fire of a Civill warre.

Sometimes also in the meerly Civill government, there be more than one Soule: As when the Power of levying mony, (which is the Nutritive faculty,) has depended on a generall Assembly; the Power of conduct and command, (which is the Motive faculty,) on one man; and the Power of making Lawes, (which is the Rationall faculty,) on the accidentall consent, not onely of those two, but also of a third; This endangereth the Common-wealth, somtimes for want of consent to good Lawes; but most often for want of such Nourishment, as is necessary to Life, and Motion. For although few perceive, that such government, is not government, but division of the Common-wealth into three Factions, and call it mixt Monarchy; yet the truth is, that it is not one independent Common-wealth, but three independent Factions; nor one Representative Person, but three. In the Kingdome of God, there may be three Persons independent, without breach of unity in God that Reigneth; but where men Reigne, that be subject to diversity of opinions, it cannot be so. And therefore if the King bear the person of the People, and the generall Assembly bear also the person of the People, and another Assembly bear the person of a Part of the people, they are not one Person, nor one Soveraign, but three Persons, and three Soveraigns.

To what Disease in the Naturall Body of man, I may exactly compare this irregularity of a Common-wealth, I know not. But I have seen a man, that had another man growing out of his side, with an head, armes, breast, and stomach, of his own: If he had had another man growing out of his other side, the comparison might then have been exact.

Hitherto I have named such Diseases of a Common-wealth, as are of the greatest, and most present danger. There be other, not so great; which neverthelesse are not unfit to be observed. As first, the difficulty of raising Mony, for the necessary uses of the Common-wealth; especially in the approach of warre. This difficulty ariseth from the opinion, that every Subject hath of a Propriety in his lands and goods, exclusive of the Soveraigns Right to the use of the same. From whence it commeth to passe, that the Soveraign Power, which foreseeth the necessities and dangers of the Common-wealth, (finding the passage of mony to the publique Treasure obstructed, by the tenacity of the people,) whereas it ought to extend it selfe, to encounter, and prevent such dangers in their beginnings, contracteth it selfe as long as it can, and when it cannot longer, struggles with the people by stratagems of Law, to obtain little summes, which not sufficing, he is fain at last violently to open the way for present supply, or Perish; and being put often to these extremities, at last reduceth the people to their due temper; or else the Common-wealth must perish. Inso-much as we may compare this Distemper very aptly to an Ague; wherein, the fleshy parts being congealed, or by venomous matter obstructed; the Veins which by their naturall course empty themselves into the Heart, are not (as they ought to be) supplyed from the Arteries, whereby there succeedeth at first a cold contraction, and trembling of the limbes; and afterwards a hot, and strong endeavour of the Heart, to force a passage for the Bloud; and before it can do that, contenteth it selfe with the small refreshments of such things as coole for a time, till (if Nature be strong enough) it break at last the contu-macy of the parts obstructed, and dissipateth the venome into sweat; or (if Nature be too weak) the Patient dyeth.

Again, there is sometimes in a Common-wealth, a Disease, which resembleth the Pleurisie; and that is, when the Treasure of the Common-wealth, flowing out of its due course, is gathered together in too much abundance, in one, or a few private men, by Monopolies, or by Farmes of the Publique Revenues; in the same manner as the Blood in a Pleurisie, getting into the Membrane of the breast, breedeth there an Inflam-mation, accompanied with a Fever, and painfull stiches.

Also, the Popularity of a potent Subject, (unlesse the Common-wealth have very good caution of his fidelity,) is a dangerous Disease; because the people (which should receive their motion from the Authority of the Sov-eraign,) by the flattery, and by the reputation of an ambitious man, are drawn away from their obedience to the Lawes, to follow a man, of whose vertues, and designes they have no knowledge. And this is commonly of more danger in a Popular Government, than in a Monarchy; because an Army is of so great force, and multitude, as it may easily be made believe, they are the People. By this means it was, that *Julius Cæsar*, who was set up by the People against the Senate, having won to himselfe the affections of his Army, made himselfe Master, both of Senate and People. And this proceeding of popular, and ambitious men, is plain Rebellion; and may be resembled to the effects of Witchcraft.

Another infirmity of a Common-wealth, is the immoderate greatnesse of a Town, when it is able to furnish out of its own Circuit, the number, and expence of a great Army: As also the great number of Corporations; which are as it were many lesser Common-wealths in the bowels of a greater, like wormes in the entrayles of a naturall man. To which may be added, the Liberty of Disputing against absolute Power, by pretenders to Politicall Prudence; which though bred for the most part in the Lees of the people; yet animated by False Doctrines, are perpetually medling with the Fundamentall Lawes, to the molestation of the Common-wealth; like the little Wormes, which Physicians call *Ascarides*.

We may further adde, the insatiable appetite, or *Bulimia*, of enlarging Dominion; with the incurable *Wounds* thereby many times received from the enemy; And the *Wens*, of ununited conquests, which are many times a burthen, and with lesse danger lost, than kept; As also the *Lethargy* of Ease, and *Consumption* of Riot and Vain Expence.

Lastly, when in a warre (forraign, or intestine,) the enemies get a final Victory; so as (the forces of the

Common-wealth keeping the field no longer) there is no farther protection of Subjects in their loyalty; then is the Common-wealth DISSOLVED, and every man at liberty to protect himselfe by such courses as his own discretion shall suggest unto him. For the Soveraign, is the publique Soule, giving Life and Motion to the Common-wealth; which expiring, the Members are governed by it no more, than the Carcasse of a man, by his departed (though Immortall) Soule. For though the Right of a Soveraign Monarch cannot be extinguished by the act of another; yet the Obligation of the members may. For he that wants protection, may seek it anywhere; and when he hath it, is obliged (without fraudulent pretence of having submitted himselfe out of fear,) to protect his Protection as long as he is able. But when the Power of an Assembly is once suppressed, the Right of the same perisheth utterly; because the Assembly it selfe is extinct; and consequently, there is no possibility for the Soveraignty to re-enter.

[. . .]

Of the Kingdome of Darknesse

Of DARKNESSE from VAIN PHILOSOPHY, and FABULOUS TRADITIONS

By PHILOSOPHY, is understood *the Knowledge acquired by Reasoning, from the Manner of the Generation of any thing, to the Properties; or from the Properties, to some possible Way of Generation of the same; to the end to bee able to produce, as far as matter, and humane force permit, such Effects, as humane life requireth.* So the Geometrician, from the Construction of Figures, findeth out many Properties thereof; and from the Properties, new Ways of their Construction, by Reasoning; to the end to be able to measure Land, and Water; and for infinite other uses. So the Astronomer, from the Rising, Setting, and Moving of the Sun, and Starres, in divers parts of the Heavens, findeth out the Causes of Day, and Night, and of the different Seasons of the Year; whereby he keepeth an account of Time: And the like of other Sciences.

By which Definition it is evident, that we are not to account as any part thereof, that originall knowledge called Experience, in which consisteth Prudence: Because it is not attained by Reasoning, but found as well in Brute Beasts, as in Man; and is but a Memory of successions of events in times past, wherein the omission of every little circumstance altering the effect, frustrateth the expectation of the most Prudent: whereas nothing is produced by Reasoning aright, but generall, eternall, and immutable Truth.

Nor are we therefore to give that name to any false Conclusions: For he that Reasoneth aright in words he understandeth, can never conclude an Error:

Nor to that which any man knows by supernaturall Revelation; because it is not acquired by Reasoning:

Nor that which is gotten by Reasoning from the Authority of Books; because it is not by Reasoning from the Cause to the Effect, nor from the Effect to the Cause; and is not Knowledg, but Faith.

The faculty of Reasoning being consequent to the use of Speech, it was not possible, but that there should have been some generall Truthes found out by Reasoning, as ancient almost as Language it selfe. The Savages of America, are not without some good Morall Sentences; also they have a little Arithmetick, to adde, and divide in Numbers not too great: but they are not therefore Philosophers. For as there were Plants of Corn and Wine in small quantity dispersed in the Fields and Woods, before men knew their vertue, or made use of them for their nourishment, or planted them apart in Fields, and Vineyards; in which time they fed on Akorns, and drank Water: so also there have been divers true, generall, and profitable Speculations from the beginning; as being the naturall plants of humane Reason: But they were at first but few in number; men lived upon grosse Experience; there was no Method; that is to say, no Sowing, nor Planting of Knowledge by it self, apart from the Weeds, and common Plants of Errour and Conjecture: And the cause of it being the want of leasure from procuring the necessities of life, and defending themselves against their neighbors, it was impossible, till the erecting of great Common-wealths, it should be otherwise. *Leasure* is the mother of *Philosophy*; and *Common-wealth*, the mother of *Peace*, and *Leasure*: Where first were great and flourishing *Cities*, there was first the study of *Philosophy*. The *Gymnosophists* of *India*, the *Magi* of *Persia*, and the *Priests* of *Chaldæa* and *Egypt*, are counted the most ancient Philosophers; and those Countreys were the most ancient of Kingdomes. *Philosophy* was not risen to the *Græcians*, and other people of the West, whose *Commonwealths* (no greater perhaps then *Lucca*, or *Geneva*) had never *Peace*, but when their fears of one another were equall; nor the *Leasure* to observe any thing but one another. At length, when Warre had united many of these *Græcian* lesser Cities, into fewer, and greater; then began *Seven men*, of severall parts of *Greece*, to get the reputation of being *Wise*; some of them for *Morall* and *Politique* Sentences; and others for the learning of the *Chaldæans* and *Egyptians*, which was *Astronomy*, and *Geometry*. But we hear not yet of any *Schools* of *Philosophy*.

After the *Athenians* by the overthrow of the *Persian* Armies, had gotten the Dominion of the Sea; and thereby, of all the Islands, and Maritime Cities of the *Archipelago*, as well of *Asia* as *Europe*; and were grown wealthy; they that had no employment, neither at home, nor abroad, had little else to employ themselves in, but either (as St. *Luke* says, *Acts* 17.21.) *in telling and hearing news*, or in discoursing of *Philosophy* publiquely to the youth of the City. Every Master took some place for that purpose. *Plato* in certain publique Walks called *Academia*, from one *Academus*: *Aristotle* in the Walk of the Temple of *Pan*, called *Lycæum*: others in the *Stoa*, or covered Walk, wherein the Merchants Goods were brought to land: others in other places; where they spent the time of their Leasure, in teaching or in disputing of their Opinions: and some in any place, where they could get the youth of the City together to hear them talk. And this was it which *Carneades* also did at *Rome*, when he was Ambassadour: which caused *Cato* to advise the Senate to dispatch him quickly, for feare of corrupting the manners of the young men that delighted to hear him speak (as they thought) fine things.

From this it was, that the place where any of them taught, and disputed, was called *Schola*, which in their Tongue signifieth *Leasure*; and their Disputations, *Diatribæ*, that is to say, *Passing of the time*. Also the Philosophers themselves had the name of their Sects, some of them from these their Schools: For they that followed *Plato*'s Doctrine, were called *Academiques*; The followers of *Aristotle*, *Peripatetiques*, from the Walk hee taught in; and those that *Zeno* taught, *Stoiques*, from the *Stoa*: as if we should denominate men from *More-fields*, from *Pauls-Church*, and from the *Exchange*, because they meet there often, to prate and loyter.

Neverthelesse, men were so much taken with this custome, that in time it spread it selfe over all Europe, and the best part of Afrique; so as there were Schools publiquely erected, and maintained for Lectures, and Disputations, almost in every Common-wealth.

There were also Schools, anciently, both before, and

after the time of our Saviour, amongst the *Jews*: but they were Schools of their Law. For though they were called *Synagogues*, that is to say, Congregations of the People; yet in as much as the Law was every Sabbath day read, expounded, and disputed in them, they differed not in nature, but in name onely from Publique Schools; and were not onely in Jerusalem, but in every City of the Gentiles, where the Jews inhabited. There was such a Schoole at *Damascus*, whereinto *Paul* entred, to persecute. There were others at *Antioch*, *Iconium* and *Thessalonica*, whereinto he entred, to dispute: And such was the Synagogue of the *Libertines*, *Cyrenians*, *Alexandrians*, *Cilicians*, and those of *Asia*; that is to say, the Schoole of *Libertines*, and of *Jewes*, that were strangers in *Jerusalem*: And of this Schoole they were that disputed (*Act.* 6.9.) with *Saint Steven*.

But what has been the Utility of those Schools? what Science is there at this day acquired by their Readings and Disputings? That wee have of Geometry, which is the Mother of all Naturall Science, wee are not indebted for it to the Schools. *Plato* that was the best Philosopher of the Greeks, forbad entrance into his Schoole, to all that were not already in some measure Geometricians. There were many that studied that Science to the great advantage of mankind: but there is no mention of their Schools; nor was there any Sect of Geometricians; nor did they then passe under the name of Philosophers. The naturall Philosophy of those Schools, was rather a Dream than Science, and set forth in senselesse and insignificant Language; which cannot be avoided by those that will teach Philosophy, without having first attained great knowledge in Geometry: For Nature worketh by Motion; the Wayes, and Degrees whereof cannot be known, without the knowledge of the Proportions and Properties of Lines, and Figures. Their Morall Philosophy is but a description of their own Passions. For the rule of Manners, without Civill Government, is the Law of Nature; and in it, the Law Civill; that determineth what is *Honest*, and *Dishonest*; what is *Just*, and *Unjust*; and generally what is *Good*, and *Evill*: whereas they make the Rules of *Good*, and *Bad*, by their own *Liking*, and *Disliking*: By which means, in so great diversity of taste, there is nothing generally agreed on; but every one doth (as far as he dares) whatsoever seemeth good in his owne eyes, to the subversion of Common-wealth. Their *Logique* which should bee the Method of Reasoning, is nothing else but Captions of Words, and Inventions how to puzzle such as should goe about to pose them. To conclude, there is nothing so absurd, that the old Philosophers (as *Cicero* saith, who was one of them) have not some of them maintained. And I beleeve that scarce any thing can be more absurdly said in naturall Philosophy, than that which now is called *Aristotles Metaphysiques*; nor more repugnant to Government, than much of that hee hath said in his *Politiques*; nor more ignorantly, than a great part of his *Ethiques*.

The Schoole of the Jews, was originally a Schoole of the Law of *Moses*; who commanded (*Deut.* 31.10.) that at the end of every seventh year, at the Feast of the Tabernacles, it should be read to all the people, that they might hear, and learn it: Therefore the reading of the Law (which was in use after the Captivity) every Sabbath day, ought to have had no other end, but the acquainting of the people with the Commandements which they were to obey, and to expound unto them the writings of the Prophets. But it is manifest, by the many reprehensions of them by our Saviour, that they corrupted the Text of the Law with their false Commentaries, and vain Traditions; and so little understood the Prophets, that they did neither acknowledge Christ, nor the works he did; of which the Prophets prophecyed. So that by their Lectures and Disputations in their Synagogues, they turned the Doctrine of their Law into a Phantasticall kind of Philosophy, concerning the incomprehensible nature of God, and of Spirits; which they compounded of the Vain Philosophy and Theology of the Græcians, mingled with their own fancies, drawn from the obscurer places of the Scripture, and which might most easily bee wrested to their purpose; and from the Fabulous Traditions of their Ancestors.

That which is now called an *University*, is a Joyning together, and an Incorporation under one Government of many Publique Schools, in one and the same Town or City. In which, the principall Schools were ordained for the three Professions, that is to say, of the Romane Religion, of the Romane Law, and of the Art of Medicine. And for the study of Philosophy it hath no otherwise place, then as a handmaid to the Romane Religion: And since the Authority of Aristotle is onely current there, that study is not properly Philosophy, (the nature whereof dependeth not on Authors,) but Aristotelity. And for Geometry, till of very late times it had no place at all; as being subservient to nothing but rigide Truth.

And if any man by the ingenuity of his owne nature, had attained to any degree of perfection therein, hee was commonly thought a Magician, and his Art Diabolicall.

Now to descend to the particular Tenets of Vain Philosophy, derived to the Universities, and thence into the Church, partly from Aristotle, partly from Blindnesse of understanding; I shall first consider their Principles. There is a certain *Philosophia prima*, on which all other Philosophy ought to depend; and consisteth principally, in right limiting of the significations of such Appellations, or Names, as are of all others the most Universall: Which Limitations serve to avoid ambiguity, and æquivocation in Reasoning; and are commonly called Definitions; such as are the Definitions of Body, Time, Place, Matter, Forme, Essence, Subject, Substance, Accident, Power, Act, Finite, Infinite, Quantity, Quality, Motion, Action, Passion, and divers others, necessary to the explaining of a mans Conceptions concerning the Nature and Generation of Bodies. The Explication (that is, the setling of the meaning) of which, and the like Terms, is commonly in the Schools called *Metaphysiques*; as being a part of the Philosophy of Aristotle, which hath that for title: but it is in another sense; for there it signifieth as much, as *Books written, or placed after his naturall Philosophy*: But the Schools take them for *Books of supernaturall Philosophy*: for the word *Metaphysiques* will bear both these senses. And indeed that which is there written, is for the most part so far from the possibility of being understood, and so repugnant to naturall Reason, that whosoever thinketh there is any thing to bee understood by it, must needs think it supernaturall.

From these Metaphysiques, which are mingled with the Scripture to make Schoole Divinity, wee are told, there be in the world certaine Essences separated from Bodies, which they call *Abstract Essences, and Substantiall Formes*: For the Interpreting of which *Jargon*, there is need of somewhat more than ordinary attention in this place. Also I ask pardon of those that are not used to this kind of Discourse, for applying my selfe to those that are. The World, (I mean not the Earth onely, that denominates the Lovers of it *Worldly men*, but the *Universe*, that is, the whole masse of all things that are) is Corporeall, that is to say, Body; and hath the dimensions of Magnitude, namely, Length, Bredth, and Depth: also every part of Body, is likewise Body, and hath the like dimensions; and consequently every part of the Universe, is Body, and that which is not Body, is no part of the Universe: And because the Universe is All, that which is no part of it, is *Nothing*; and consequently *no where*. Nor does it follow from hence, that Spirits are *nothing*: for they have dimensions, and are therefore really *Bodies*; though that name in common Speech be given to such Bodies onely, as are visible, or palpable; that is, that have some degree of Opacity: But for Spirits, they call them Incorporeall; which is a name of more honour, and may therefore with more piety bee attributed to God himselfe; in whom wee consider not what Attribute expresseth best his Nature, which is Incomprehensible; but what best expresseth our desire to honour Him.

To know now upon what grounds they say there be *Essences Abstract*, or *Substantiall Formes*, wee are to consider what those words do properly signifie. The use of Words, is to register to our selves, and make manifest to others the Thoughts and Conceptions of our Minds. Of which Words, some are the names of the Things conceived; as the names of all sorts of Bodies, that work upon the Senses, and leave an Impression in the Imagination: Others are the names of the Imaginations themselves; that is to say, of those Ideas, or mentall Images we have of all things wee see, or remember: And others againe are names of Names; or of different sorts of Speech: As *Universall, Plurall, Singular, are the names of Names; and Definition, Affirmation, Negation, True, False, Syllogisme, Interrogation, Promise, Covenant,* are the names of certain Forms of Speech. Others serve to shew the Consequence, or Repugnance of one name to another; as when one saith, *A Man is a Body,* hee intendeth that the name of *Body* is necessarily consequent to the name of *Man;* as being but severall names of the same thing, *Man;* which Consequence is signified by coupling them together with the word *Is.* And as wee use the Verbe *Is;* so the Latines use their Verbe *Est,* and the Greeks their Ἔστι through all its Declinations. Whether all other Nations of the world have in their severall languages a word that answereth to it, or not, I cannot tell; but I am sure they have not need of it: For the placing of two names in order may serve to signifie their Consequence, if it were the custome, (for Custome is it, that give words their force,) as well as the words *Is,* or *Bee,* or *Are,* and the like.

And if it were so, that there were a Language without any Verb answerable to *Est,* or *Is,* or *Bee;* yet the men that used it would bee not a jot the lesse capable of

Inferring, Concluding, and of all kind of Reasoning, than were the Greeks, and Latines. But what then would become of these Terms, of *Entity*, *Essence*, *Essentiall*, *Essentiality*, that are derived from it, and of many more that depend on these, applyed as most commonly they are? They are therefore no Names of Things; but Signes, by which wee make known, that wee conceive the Consequence of one name or Attribute to another: as when we say, *a Man, is, a living Body*, wee mean not that the *Man* is one thing, the *Living Body* another, and the *Is*, or *Beeing* a third: but that the *Man*, and the *Living Body*, is the same thing: because the Consequence, *If hee bee a Man, hee is a living Body*, is a true Consequence, signified by that word *Is*. Therefore, *to bee a Body, to Walke, to bee Speaking, to Live, to See*, and the like Infinitives; also *Corporeity, Walking, Speaking, Life, Sight*, and the like, that signifie just the same, are the names of *Nothing*; as I have elsewhere more amply expressed.

But to what purpose (may some man say) is such subtilty in a work of this nature, where I pretend to nothing but what is necessary to the doctrine of Government and Obedience? It is to this purpose, that men may no longer suffer themselves to be abused, by them, that by this doctrine of *Separated Essences*, built on the Vain Philosophy of Aristotle, would fright them from Obeying the Laws of their Countrey, with empty names; as men fright Birds from the Corn with an empty doublet, a hat, and a crooked stick. For it is upon this ground, that when a Man is dead and buried, they say his Soule (that is his Life) can walk separated from his Body, and is seen by night amongst the graves. Upon the same ground they say, that the Figure, and Colour, and Tast of a peece of Bread, has a being, there, where they say there is no Bread: And upon the same ground they say, that Faith, and Wisdome, and other Vertues are sometimes *powred* into a man, sometimes *blown* into him from Heaven; as if the Vertuous, and their Vertues could be asunder; and a great many other things that serve to lessen the dependence of Subjects on the Soveraign Power of their Countrey. For who will endeavour to obey the Laws, if he expect Obedience to be Powred or Blown into him? Or who will not obey a Priest, that can make God, rather than his Soveraign; nay than God himselfe? Or who, that is in fear of Ghosts, will not bear great respect to those that can make the Holy Water, that drives them from him? And this shall suffice for an example of the Errors, which are brought into the Church, from the *Entities*, and *Essences* of Aristotle: which it may be he knew to be false Philosophy; but writ it as a thing consonant to, and corroborative of their Religion; and fearing the fate of Socrates.

Being once fallen into this Error of *Separated Essences*, they are thereby necessarily involved in many other absurdities that follow it. For seeing they will have these Forms to be reall, they are obliged to assign them *some place*. But because they hold them Incorporeall, without all dimension of Quantity, and all men know that Place is Dimension, and not to be filled, but by that which is Corporeall; they are driven to uphold their credit with a distinction, that they are not indeed any where *Circumscriptivè*, but *Definitive*: Which Terms being meer Words, and in this occasion insignificant, passe onely in Latine, that the vanity of them may bee concealed. For the Circumscription of a thing, is nothing else but the Determination, or Defining of its Place; and so both the Terms of the Distinction are the same. And in particular, of the Essence of a Man, which (they say) is his Soule, they affirm it, to be All of it in his little Finger, and All of it in every other Part (how small soever) of his Body; and yet no more Soule in the Whole Body, than in any one of those Parts. Can any man think that God is served with such absurdities? And yet all this is necessary to beleeve, to those that will beleeve the Existence of an Incorporeall Soule, Separated from the Body.

And when they come to give account, how an Incorporeall Substance can be capable of Pain, and be tormented in the fire of Hell, or Purgatory, they have nothing at all to answer, but that it cannot be known how fire can burn Soules.

Again, whereas Motion is change of Place, and Incorporeall Substances are not capable of Place, they are troubled to make it seem possible, how a Soule can goe hence, without the Body to Heaven, Hell, or Purgatory; and how the Ghosts of men (and I may adde of their clothes which they appear in) can walk by night in Churches, Churchyards, and other places of Sepulture. To which I know not what they can answer, unlesse they will say, they walke *definitivè*, not *circumscriptivè*, or *spiritually*, not *temporally*: for such egregious distinctions are equally applicable to any difficulty whatsoever.

For the meaning of *Eternity*, they will not have it to be an Endlesse Succession of Time; for then they should not be able to render a reason how Gods Will, and

Præordaining of things to come, should not be before his Præscience of the same, as the Efficient Cause before the Effect, or Agent before the Action; nor of many other their bold opinions concerning the Incomprehensible Nature of God. But they will teach us, that Eternity is the Standing still of the Present Time, a *Nunc-stans* (as the Schools call it;) which neither they, nor any else understand, no more than they would a *Hic-stans* for an Infinite greatnesse of Place.

And whereas men divide a Body in their thought, by numbring parts of it, and in numbring those parts, number also the parts of the Place it filled; it cannot be, but in making many parts, wee make also many places of those parts; whereby there cannot bee conceived in the mind of any man, more, or fewer parts, than there are places for: yet they will have us beleeve, that by the Almighty power of God, one body may be at one and the same time in many places; and many bodies at one and the same time in one place; as if it were an acknowledgment of the Divine Power, to say, that which is, is not; or that which has been, has not been. And these are but a small part of the Incongruities they are forced to, from their disputing Philosophically, in stead of admiring, and adoring of the Divine and Incomprehensible Nature; whose Attributes cannot signifie what he is, but ought to signifie our desire to honour him, with the best Appellations we can think on. But they that venture to reason of his Nature, from these Attributes of Honour, losing their understanding in the very first attempt, fall from one Inconvenience into another, without end, and without number; in the same manner, as when a man ignorant of the Ceremonies of Court, comming into the presence of a greater Person than he is used to speak to, and stumbling at his entrance, to save himselfe from falling, lets slip his Cloake; to recover his Cloake, lets fall his Hat; and with one disorder after another, discovers his astonishment and rusticity.

Then for *Physiques*, that is, the knowledge of the subordinate, and secundary causes of naturall events; they render none at all, but empty words. If you desire to know why some kind of bodies sink naturally downwards toward the Earth, and others goe naturally from it; The Schools will tell you out of Aristotle, that the bodies that sink downwards, are *Heavy*; and that this Heavinesse is it that causes them to descend: But if you ask what they mean by *Heavinesse*, they will define it to bee an endeavour to goe to the center of the Earth: so that the cause why things sink downward, is an Endeavour to be below: which is as much as to say, that bodies descend, or ascend, because they doe. Or they will tell you the center of the Earth is the place of Rest, and Conservation for Heavy things; and therefore they endeavour to be there: As if Stones, and Metalls had a desire, or could discern the place they would bee at, as Man does; or loved Rest, as Man does not; or that a peece of Glasse were lesse safe in the Window, than falling into the Street.

If we would know why the same Body seems greater (without adding to it) one time, than another; they say, when it seems lesse, it is *Condensed*; when greater, *Rarefied*. What is that *Condensed*, and *Rarefied*? Condensed, is when there is in the very same Matter, lesse

Quantity than before; and Rarefied, when more. As if there could be Matter, that had not some determined Quantity; when Quantity is nothing else but the Determination of Matter; that is to say of Body, by which we say one Body is greater, or lesser than another, by thus, or thus much. Or as if a Body were made without any Quantity at all, and that afterwards more, or lesse were put into it, according as it is intended the Body should be more, or lesse Dense.

For the cause of the Soule of Man, they say, *Creatur Infundendo*, and *Creando Infunditur*: that is, *It is Created by Powring it in*, and *Powred in by Creation*.

For the Cause of Sense, an ubiquity of *Species*; that is, of the *Shews* or *Apparitions* of objects; which when they be Apparitions to the Eye, is *Sight*; when to the Eare, *Hearing*; to the Palate, *Tast*; to the Nostrill, *Smelling*; and to the rest of the Body, *Feeling*.

For cause of the Will, to doe any particular action, which is called *Volitio*, they assign the Faculty, that is to say, the Capacity in generall, that men have, to will sometimes one thing, sometimes another, which is called *Voluntas*; making the *Power* the cause of the *Act*: As if one should assign for cause of the good or evill Acts of men, their Ability to doe them.

And in many occasions they put for cause of Naturall events, their own Ignorance, but disguised in other words: As when they say, Fortune is the cause of things contingent; that is, of things whereof they know no cause: And as when they attribute many Effects to *occult qualities*; that is, qualities not known to them; and therefore also (as they thinke) to no Man else. And to

Sympathy, Antipathy, Antiperistasis, Specificall Qualities, and other like Termes, which signifie neither the Agent that produceth them, nor the Operation by which they are produced.

If such *Metaphysiques,* and *Physiques* as this, be not *Vain Philosophy,* there was never any; nor needed St. Paul to give us warning to avoid it.

And for their Morall, and Civill Philosophy, it hath the same, or greater absurdities. If a man doe an action of Injustice, that is to say, an action contrary to the Law, God they say is the prime cause of the Law, and also the prime cause of that, and all other Actions; but no cause at all of the Injustice; which is the Inconformity of the Action to the Law. This is Vain Philosophy. A man might as well say, that one man maketh both a streight line, and a crooked, and another maketh their Incongruity. And such is the Philosophy of all men that resolve of their Conclusions, before they know their Premises; pretending to comprehend, that which is Incomprehensible; and of Attributes of Honour to make Attributes of Nature; as this distinction was made to maintain the Doctrine of Free-Will, that is, of a Will of man, not subject to the Will of God.

Aristotle, and other Heathen Philosophers define Good, and Evill, by the Appetite of men; and well enough, as long as we consider them governed every one by his own Law: For in the condition of men that have no other Law but their own Appetites, there can be no generall Rule of Good, and Evill Actions. But in a Common-wealth this measure is false: Not the Appetite of Private men, but the Law, which is the Will and

Appetite of the State is the measure. And yet is this Doctrine still practised; and men judge the Goodnesse, or Wickednesse of their own, and of other mens actions, and of the actions of the Common-wealth it selfe, by their own Passions; and no man calleth Good or Evill, but that which is so in his own eyes, without any regard at all to the Publique Laws; except onely Monks, and Friers, that are bound by Vow to that simple obedience to their Superiour, to which every Subject ought to think himself bound by the Law of Nature to the Civill Soveraign. And this private measure of Good, is a Doctrine, not onely Vain, but also Pernicious to the Publique State.

It is also Vain and false Philosophy, to say the work of Marriage is repugnant to Chastity, or Continence, and by consequence to make them Morall Vices; as they doe, that pretend Chastity, and Continence, for the ground of denying Marriage to the Clergy. For they confesse it is no more, but a Constitution of the Church, that requireth in those holy Orders that continually attend the Altar, and administration of the Eucharist, a continuall Abstinence from women, under the name of continuall Chastity, Continence, and Purity. Therefore they call the lawfull use of Wives, want of Chastity, and Continence; and so make Marriage a Sin, or at least a thing so impure, and unclean, as to render a man unfit for the Altar. If the Law were made because the use of Wives is Incontinence, and contrary to Chastity, then all Marriage is vice: If because it is a thing too impure, and unclean for a man consecrated to God; much more should other naturall, necessary, and daily works which all men doe, render men unworthy to bee Priests, because they are more unclean.

But the secret foundation of this prohibition of Marriage of Priests, is not likely to have been laid so slightly, as upon such errours in Morall Philosophy; nor yet upon the preference of single life, to the estate of Matrimony; which proceeded from the wisdome of St. Paul, who perceived how inconvenient a thing it was, for those that in those times of persecution were Preachers of the Gospel, and forced to fly from one countrey to another, to be clogged with the care of wife and children; but upon the designe of the Popes, and Priests of after times, to make themselves the Clergy, that is to say, sole Heirs of the Kingdome of God in this world; to which it was necessary to take from them the use of Marriage, because our Saviour saith, that at the coming of his Kingdome the Children of God *shall neither Marry, nor bee given in Marriage, but shall bee as the Angels in heaven*; that is to say, Spirituall. Seeing then they had taken on them the name of Spirituall, to have allowed themselves (when there was no need) the propriety of Wives, had been an Incongruity.

From Aristotles Civill Philosophy, they have learned, to call all manner of Common-wealths but the Popular, (such as was at that time the state of Athens,) *Tyranny*. All Kings they called Tyrants; and the Aristocracy of the thirty Governours set up there by the Lacedemonians that subdued them, the thirty Tyrants: As also to call the condition of the people under the Democracy, *Liberty*. A *Tyrant* originally signified no more simply, but a *Monarch*: But when afterwards in most parts of Greece that kind of government was abolished, the name began to signifie, not onely the thing it did before, but with it, the hatred which the Popular States bare towards it: As also the name of King became odious after the deposing of the Kings in Rome, as being a thing naturall to all men, to conceive some great Fault to be signified in any Attribute, that is given in despight, and to a great Enemy. And when the same men shall be displeased with those that have the administration of the Democracy, or Aristocracy, they are not to seek for disgracefull names to expresse their anger in; but call readily the one *Anarchy*, and the other, *Oligarchy*, or the *Tyranny of a Few*. And that which offendeth the People, is no other thing, but that they are governed, not as every one of them would himselfe, but as the Publique Representant, be it one Man, or an Assembly of men thinks fit; that is, by an Arbitrary government: for which they give evill names to their Superiors; never knowing (till perhaps a little after a Civill warre) that without such Arbitrary government, such Warre must be perpetuall; and that it is Men, and Arms, not Words, and Promises, that make the Force and Power of the Laws.

And therefore this is another Errour of Aristotles Politiques, that in a wel ordered Common-wealth, not Men should govern, but the Laws. What man, that has his naturall Senses, though he can neither write nor read, does not find himself governed by them he fears, and beleeves can kill or hurt him when he obeyeth not? or that beleeves the Law can hurt him; that is, Words, and Paper, without the Hands, and Swords of men? And this is of the number of pernicious Errors: for they induce men, as oft as they like not their Governours, to adhære to those that call them Tyrants, and to think it lawfull to raise warre against them: And yet they are many times cherished from the Pulpit, by the Clergy.

There is another Errour in their Civill Philosophy (which they never learned of Aristotle, nor Cicero, nor any other of the Heathen,) to extend the power of the Law, which is the Rule of Actions onely, to the very Thoughts, and Consciences of men, by Examination, and *Inquisition* of what they Hold, notwithstanding the Conformity of their Speech and Actions: By which, men are either punished for answering the truth of their thoughts, or constrained to answer an untruth for fear of punishment. It is true, that the Civill Magistrate, intending to employ a Minister in the charge of Teaching, may enquire of him, if hee bee content to Preach such, and such Doctrines; and in case of refusall, may deny him the employment: But to force him to accuse himselfe of Opinions, when his Actions are not by Law forbidden, is against the Law of Nature; and especially in them, who teach, that a man shall bee damned to Eternall and extream torments, if he die in a false opinion concerning an Article of the Christian Faith. For who is there, that knowing there is so great danger in an error, whom the naturall care of himself, compelleth not to hazard his Soule upon his own judgement, rather than that of any other man that is unconcerned in his damnation?

For a Private man, without the Authority of the Common-wealth, that is to say, without permission from the Representant thereof, to Interpret the Law by his own Spirit, is another Error in the Politiques; but not drawn from Aristotle, nor from any other of the Heathen Philosophers. For none of them deny, but that in the Power of making Laws, is comprehended also the Power of Explaining them when there is need. And are not the Scriptures, in all places where they are Law, made Law by the Authority of the Common-wealth, and consequently, a part of the Civill Law?

Of the same kind it is also, when any but the Soveraign restraineth in any man that power which the Common-wealth hath not restrained; as they do, that impropriate the Preaching of the Gospell to one certain Order of men, where the Laws have left it free. If the State give me leave to preach, or teach; that is, if it forbid me not, no man can forbid me. If I find my selfe amongst the Idolaters of America, shall I that am a Christian, though not in Orders, think it a sin to preach Jesus Christ, till I have received Orders from Rome? or when I have preached, shall not I answer their doubts, and expound the Scriptures to them; that is, shall I not Teach? But for this may some say, as also for administring to them the Sacraments, the necessity shall be esteemed for a sufficient Mission; which is true: But this is true also, that for whatsoever, a dispensation is due for the necessity, for the same there needs no dispensation, when there is no Law that forbids it. Therefore to deny these Functions to those, to whom the Civill Soveraigne hath not denied them, is a taking away of a lawfull Liberty, which is contrary to the Doctrine of Civill Government.

More examples of Vain Philosophy, brought into Religion by the Doctors of Schoole-Divinity, might be produced; but other men may if they please observe them of themselves. I shall onely adde this, that the Writings of Schoole-Divines, are nothing else for the most part, but insignificant Traines of strange and barbarous words, or words otherwise used, then in the common use of the Latine tongue; such as would pose Cicero, and Varro, and all the Grammarians of ancient Rome. Which if any man would see proved, let him (as I have said once before) see whether he can translate any Schoole-Divine into any of the Modern tongues, as French, English, or any other copious language: for that which cannot in most of these be made Intelligible, is not Intelligible in the Latine. Which Insignificancy of language, though I cannot note it for false Philosophy; yet it hath a quality, not onely to hide the Truth, but also to make men think they have it, and desist from further search.

Lastly, for the Errors brought in from false, or uncertain History, what is all the Legend of fictitious Miracles, in the lives of the Saints; and all the Histories of Apparitions, and Ghosts, alledged by the Doctors of the Romane Church, to make good their Doctrines of Hell, and Purgatory, the power of Exorcisme, and other Doctrines which have no warrant, neither in Reason, nor Scripture; as also all those Traditions which they call the unwritten Word of God; but old Wives Fables? Whereof, though they find dispersed somewhat in the Writings of the ancient Fathers; yet those Fathers were men, that might too easily beleeve false reports; and the producing of their opinions for testimony of the truth of what they beleeved, hath no other force with them that (according to the Counsell of St. *John* 1 Epist. chap. 4. verse 1.)

examine Spirits, than in all things that concern the power of the Romane Church, (the abuse whereof either they suspected not, or had benefit by it,) to discredit their testimony, in respect of too rash beleef of reports; which the most sincere men, without great knowledge of naturall causes, (such as the Fathers were) are commonly the most subject to: For naturally, the best men are the least suspicious of fraudulent purposes. Gregory the Pope, and S. Bernard have somewhat of Apparitions of Ghosts, that said they were in Purgatory; and so has our Beda: but no where, I beleeve, but by report from others. But if they, or any other, relate any such stories of their own knowledge, they shall not thereby confirm the more such vain reports; but discover their own Infirmity, or Fraud.

With the Introduction of False, we may joyn also the suppression of True Philosophy, by such men, as neither by lawfull authority, nor sufficient study, are competent Judges of the truth. Our own Navigations make manifest, and all men learned in humane Sciences, now acknowledge there are Antipodes: And every day it appeareth more and more, that Years, and Dayes are determined by Motions of the Earth. Neverthelesse, men that have in their Writings but supposed such Doctrine, as an occasion to lay open the reasons for, and against it, have been punished for it by Authority Ecclesiasticall. But what reason is there for it? Is it because such opinions are contrary to true Religion? that cannot be, if they be true. Let therefore the truth be first examined by competent Judges, or confuted by them that pretend to know the contrary. Is it because they be contrary to the

Religion established? Let them be silenced by the Laws of those, to whom the Teachers of them are subject; that is, by the Laws Civill: For disobedience may lawfully be punished in them, that against the Laws teach even true Philosophy. Is it because they tend to disorder in Government, as countenancing Rebellion, or Sedition? then let them be silenced, and the Teachers punished by vertue of his Power to whom the care of the Publique quiet is committed; which is the Authority Civill. For whatsoever Power Ecclesiastiques take upon themselves (in any place where they are subject to the State) in their own Right, though they call it Gods Right, is but Usurpation.

Of the BENEFIT *that proceedeth from such Darknesse, and to whom it accreweth*

Cicero maketh honorable mention of one of the *Cassii*, a severe Judge amongst the Romans, for a custome he had, in Criminall causes, (when the testimony of the witnesses was not sufficient,) to ask the Accusers, *Cui bono*; that is to say, what Profit, Honor, or other Contentment, the accused obtained, or expected by the Fact. For amongst Præsumptions, there is none that so evidently declareth the Author, as doth the BENEFIT of the Action. By the same rule I intend in this place to examine, who they may be, that have possessed the People so long in this part of Christendome, with these Doctrines, contrary to the Peaceable Societies of Mankind.

And first, to this Error, *that the present Church now Mili-*

tant on Earth, is the Kingdome of God, (that is, the Kingdome of Glory, or the Land of Promise; not the Kingdome of Grace, which is but a Promise of the Land,) are annexed these worldly Benefits, First, that the Pastors, and Teachers of the Church, are entitled thereby, as Gods Publique Ministers, to a Right of Governing the Church; and consequently (because the Church, and Common-wealth are the same Persons) to be Rectors, and Governours of the Common-wealth. By this title it is, that the Pope prevailed with the subjects of all Christian Princes, to beleeve, that to disobey him, was to disobey Christ himselfe; and in all differences between him and other Princes, (charmed with the word *Power Spirituall*,) to abandon their lawfull Soveraigns; which is in effect an universall Monarchy over all Christendome. For though they were first invested in the right of being Supreme Teachers of Christian Doctrine, by, and under Christian Emperors, within the limits of the Romane Empire (as is acknowledged by themselves) by the title of *Pontifex Maximus*, who was an Officer subject to the Civill State; yet after the Empire was divided, and dissolved, it was not hard to obtrude upon the people already subject to them, another Title, namely, the Right of St. Peter; not onely to save entire their pretended Power; but also to extend the same over the same Christian Provinces, though no more united in the Empire of Rome. This Benefit of an Universall Monarchy, (considering the desire of men to bear Rule) is a sufficient Presumption, that the Popes that pretended to it, and for a long time enjoyed it, were the Authors of the Doctrine, by which it was obtained; namely, that the Church now on Earth, is the

Kingdome of Christ. For that granted, it must be understood, that Christ hath some Lieutenant amongst us, by whom we are to be told what are his Commandements.

After that certain Churches had renounced this universall Power of the Pope, one would expect in reason, that the Civill Soveraigns in all those Churches, should have recovered so much of it, as (before they had unadvisedly let it goe) was their own Right, and in their own hands. And in England it was so in effect; saving that they, by whom the Kings administred the Government of Religion, by maintaining their imployment to be in Gods Right, seemed to usurp, if not a Supremacy, yet an Independency on the Civill Power: and they but seemed to usurpe it, in as much as they acknowledged a Right in the King, to deprive them of the Exercise of their Functions at his pleasure.

But in those places where the Presbytery took that Office, though many other Doctrines of the Church of Rome were forbidden to be taught; yet this Doctrine, that the Kingdome of Christ is already come, and that it began at the Resurrection of our Saviour, was still retained. But *cui bono?* What Profit did they expect from it? The same which the Popes expected: to have a Soveraign Power over the People. For what is it for men to excommunicate their lawful King, but to keep him from all places of Gods publique Service in his own Kingdom? and with force to resist him, when he with force endeavoureth to correct them? Or what is it, without Authority from the Civill Soveraign, to excommunicate any person, but to take from him his Lawfull Liberty, that is, to usurpe an unlawfull Power over their Brethren? The

Authors therefore of this Darknesse in Religion, are the Romane, and the Presbyterian Clergy.

To this head, I referre also all those Doctrines, that serve them to keep the possession of this spirituall Soveraignty after it is gotten. As first, that the *Pope in his publique capacity cannot erre*. For who is there, that beleeving this to be true, will not readily obey him in whatsoever he commands?

Secondly, that all other Bishops, in what Commonwealth soever, have not their Right, neither immediately from God, nor mediately from their Civill Soveraigns, but from the Pope, is a Doctrine, by which there comes to be in every Christian Common-wealth many potent men, (for so are Bishops,) that have their dependance on the Pope, and owe obedience to him, though he be a forraign Prince; by which means he is able, (as he hath done many times) to raise a Civill War against the State that submits not it self to be governed according to his pleasure and Interest.

Thirdly, the exemption of these, and of all other Priests, and of all Monkes, and Fryers, from the Power of the Civill Laws. For by this means, there is a great part of every Common-wealth, that enjoy the benefit of the Laws, and are protected by the Power of the Civill State, which neverthelesse pay no part of the Publique expence; nor are lyable to the penalties, as other Subjects, due to their crimes; and consequently, stand not in fear of any man, but the Pope; and adhere to him onely, to uphold his universall Monarchy.

Fourthly, the giving to their Priests (which is no more in the New Testament but Presbyters, that is, Elders) the name of *Sacerdotes*, that is, Sacrificers, which was the title of the Civill Soveraign, and his publique Ministers, amongst the Jews, whilest God was their King. Also, the making the Lords Supper a Sacrifice, serveth to make the People beleeve the Pope hath the same power over all Christians, that Moses and Aaron had over the Jews; that is to say, all Power, both Civill and Ecclesiasticall, as the High Priest then had.

Fiftly, the teaching that Matrimony is a Sacrament, giveth to the Clergy the Judging of the lawfulnesse of Marriages; and thereby, of what Children are Legitimate; and consequently, of the Right of Succession to hæreditary Kingdomes.

Sixtly, the Deniall of Marriage to Priests, serveth to assure this Power of the Pope over Kings. For if a King be a Priest, he cannot Marry, and transmit his Kingdome to his Posterity; If he be not a Priest then the Pope pretendeth this Authority Ecclesiasticall over him, and over his people.

Seventhly, from Auricular Confession, they obtain, for the assurance of their Power, better intelligence of the designs of Princes, and great persons in the Civill State, than these can have of the designs of the State Ecclesiasticall.

Eighthly, by the Canonization of Saints, and declaring who are Martyrs, they assure their Power, in that they induce simple men into an obstinacy against the Laws and Commands of their Civill Soveraigns even to death, if by the Popes excommunication, they be declared Heretiques or Enemies to the Church; that is, (as they interpret it,) to the Pope.

Ninthly, they assure the same, by the Power they ascribe to every Priest, of making Christ; and by the Power of ordaining Pennance; and of Remitting, and Retaining of sins.

Tenthly, by the Doctrine of Purgatory, of Justification by externall works, and of Indulgences, the Clergy is enriched.

Eleventhly, by their Dæmonology, and the use of Exorcisme, and other things appertaining thereto, they keep (or thinke they keep) the People more in awe of their Power.

Lastly, the Metaphysiques, Ethiques, and Politiques of Aristotle, the frivolous Distinctions, barbarous Terms, and obscure Language of the Schoolmen, taught in the Universities, (which have been all erected and regulated by the Popes Authority,) serve them to keep these Errors from being detected, and to make men mistake the *Ignis fatuus* of Vain Philosophy, for the Light of the Gospell.

To these, if they sufficed not, might be added other of their dark Doctrines, the profit whereof redoundeth manifestly, to the setting up of an unlawfull Power over the lawfull Soveraigns of Christian People; or for the sustaining of the same, when it is set up; or to the worldly Riches, Honour, and Authority of those that sustain it. And therefore by the aforesaid rule, of *Cui bono*, we may justly pronounce for the Authors of all this Spirituall Darknesse, the Pope, and Roman Clergy, and all those besides that endeavour to settle in the mindes of men this erroneous Doctrine, that the Church now on Earth, is that Kingdome of God mentioned in the Old and New Testament.

But the Emperours, and other Christian Soveraigns, under whose Government these Errours, and the like encroachments of Ecclesiastiques upon their Office, at first crept in, to the disturbance of their possessions, and of the tranquillity of their Subjects, though they suffered the same for want of foresight of the Sequel, and of insight into the designs of their Teachers, may neverthelesse bee esteemed accessaries to their own, and the Publique dammage: For without their Authority there could at first no seditious Doctrine have been publiquely preached. I say they might have hindred the same in the beginning: But when the people were once possessed by those spirituall men, there was no humane remedy to be applyed, that any man could invent: And for the remedies that God should provide, who never faileth in his good time to destroy all the Machinations of men against the Truth, wee are to attend his good pleasure, that suffereth many times the prosperity of his enemies, together with their ambition, to grow to such a height, as the violence thereof openeth the eyes, which the warinesse of their predecessours had before sealed up, and makes men by too much grasping let goe all, as Peters net was broken, by the struggling of too great a multitude of Fishes; whereas the Impatience of those, that strive to resist such encroachment, before their Subjects eyes were opened, did but encrease the power they resisted. I doe not therefore blame the Emperour Frederick for holding the stirrop to our countryman Pope Adrian; for such was the disposition of his subjects then, as if hee had not done it, hee was not likely to have succeeded in the Empire: But I blame those, that in the beginning, when their power was entire, by suffering such Doctrines to be forged in the Universities of their own Dominions, have holden the Stirrop to all the succeeding Popes, whilest they mounted into the Thrones of all Christian Soveraigns, to ride, and tire, both them, and their people, at their pleasure.

But as the Inventions of men are woven, so also are they ravelled out; the way is the same, but the order is inverted: The web begins at the first Elements of Power, which are Wisdom, Humility, Sincerity, and other vertues of the Apostles, whom the people converted, obeyed, out of Reverence, not by Obligation: Their Consciences were free, and their Words and Actions subject to none but the Civill Power. Afterwards the Presbyters (as the Flocks of Christ encreased) assembling to consider what they should teach, and thereby obliging themselves to teach nothing against the Decrees of their Assemblies, made it to be thought the people were thereby obliged to follow their Doctrine, and when they refused, refused to keep them company, (that was then called Excommunication,) not as being Infidels, but as being disobedient: And this was the first knot upon their Liberty. And the number of Presbyters encreasing, the Presbyters of the chief City or Province, got themselves an authority over the Parochiall Presbyters, and appropriated to themselves the names of Bishops: And this was a second knot on Christian Liberty. Lastly, the Bishop of Rome, in regard of the Imperiall City, took upon him an Authority (partly by the wills of the Emperours themselves, and by the title of *Pontifex Maximus*, and at last when the Emperours were grown weak, by the priviledges of

St. Peter) over all other Bishops of the Empire: Which was the third and last knot, and the whole *Synthesis* and *Construction* of the Pontificall Power.

And therefore the *Analysis*, or *Resolution* is by the same way; but beginning with the knot that was last tyed; as wee may see in the dissolution of the præterpoliticall Church Government in England. First, the Power of the Popes was dissolved totally by Queen Elizabeth; and the Bishops, who before exercised their Functions in Right of the Pope, did afterwards exercise the same in Right of the Queen and her Successours; though by retaining the phrase of *Jure Divino*, they were thought to demand it by immediate Right from God: And so was untyed the first knot. After this, the Presbyterians lately in England obtained the putting down of Episcopacy: And so was the second knot dissolved: And almost at the same time, the Power was taken also from the Presbyterians: And so we are reduced to the Independency of the Primitive Christians to follow Paul, or Cephas, or Apollos, every man as he liketh best: Which, if it be without contention, and without measuring the Doctrine of Christ, by our affection to the Person of his Minister, (the fault which the Apostle reprehended in the Corinthians,) is perhaps the best: First, because there ought to be no Power over the Consciences of men, but of the Word it selfe, working Faith in every one, not alwayes according to the purpose of them that Plant and Water, but of God himself, that giveth the Increase: and secondly, because it is unreasonable in them, who teach there is such danger in every little Errour, to require of a man endued with Reason of his own, to follow the Reason of any other man, or of the most voices of many other men; Which is little better, then to venture his Salvation at crosse and pile. Nor ought those Teachers to be displeased with this losse of their antient Authority: For there is none should know better then they, that power is preserved by the same Vertues by which it is acquired; that is to say, by Wisdome, Humility, Clearnesse of Doctrine, and sincerity of Conversation; and not by suppression of the Naturall Sciences, and of the Morality of Naturall Reason; nor by obscure Language; nor by Arrogating to themselves more Knowledge than they make appear; nor by Pious Frauds; nor by such other faults, as in the Pastors of Gods Church are not only Faults, but also scandalls, apt to make men stumble one time or other upon the suppression of their Authority.

But after this Doctrine, *that the Church now Militant, is the Kingdome of God spoken of in the Old and New Testament*, was received in the World; the ambition, and canvasing for the Offices that belong thereunto, and especially for that great Office of being Christs Lieutenant, and the Pompe of them that obtained therein the principall Publique Charges, became by degrees so evident, that they lost the inward Reverence due to the Pastorall Function: in so much as the Wisest men, of them that had any power in the Civill State, needed nothing but the authority of their Princes, to deny them any further Obedience. For, from the time that the Bishop of Rome had gotten to be acknowledged for Bishop Universall, by pretence of Succession to St. Peter, their whole Hierarchy, or Kingdome of Darknesse, may be compared not unfitly to the *Kingdome of Fairies*; that is, to the old wives

Fables in England, concerning *Ghosts* and *Spirits*, and the feats they play in the night. And if a man consider the originall of this great Ecclesiasticall Dominion, he will easily perceive, that the *Papacy*, is no other, than the *Ghost* of the deceased *Romane Empire*, sitting crowned upon the grave thereof: For so did the Papacy start up on a Sudden out of the Ruines of that Heathen Power.

The *Language* also, which they use, both in the Churches, and in their Publique Acts, being *Latine*, which is not commonly used by any Nation now in the world, what is it but the *Ghost* of the Old *Romane Language*?

The *Fairies* in what Nation soever they converse, have but one Universall King, which some Poets of ours call King *Oberon*; but the Scripture calls *Beelzebub*, Prince of *Dæmons*. The *Ecclesiastiques* likewise, in whose Dominions soever they be found, acknowledge but one Universall King, the *Pope*.

The *Ecclesiastiques* are *Spirituall* men, and *Ghostly* Fathers. The Fairies are *Spirits*, and *Ghosts*. *Fairies* and *Ghosts* inhabite Darknesse, Solitudes, and Graves. The *Ecclesiastiques* walke in Obscurity of Doctrine, in Monasteries, Churches, and Churchyards.

The *Ecclesiastiques* have their Cathedral Churches; which, in what Towne soever they be erected, by vertue of Holy Water, and certain Charmes called Exorcismes, have the power to make those Townes, Cities, that is to say, Seats of Empire. The *Fairies* also have their enchanted Castles, and certain Gigantique Ghosts, that domineer over the Regions round about them.

The *Fairies* are not to be seized on; and brought to

answer for the hurt they do. So also the *Ecclesiastiques* vanish away from the Tribunals of Civill Justice.

The *Ecclesiastiques* take from young men, the use of Reason, by certain Charms compounded of Metaphysiques, and Miracles, and Traditions, and Abused Scripture, whereby they are good for nothing else, but to execute what they command them. The *Fairies* likewise are said to take young Children out of their Cradles, and to change them into Naturall Fools, which Common people do therefore call *Elves*, and are apt to mischief.

In what Shop, or Operatory the Fairies make their Enchantment, the old Wives have not determined. But the Operatories of the *Clergy*, are well enough known to be the Universities, that received their Discipline from Authority Pontificiall.

When the *Fairies* are displeased with any body, they are said to send their Elves, to pinch them. The *Ecclesiastiques*, when they are displeased with any Civill State, make also their Elves, that is, Superstitious, Enchanted Subjects, to pinch their Princes, by preaching Sedition; or one Prince enchanted with promises, to pinch another.

The *Fairies* marry not; but there be amongst them *Incubi*, that have copulation with flesh and bloud. The *Priests* also marry not.

The *Ecclesiastiques* take the Cream of the Land, by Donations of ignorant men, that stand in aw of them, and by Tythes: So also it is in the Fable of *Fairies*, that they enter into the Dairies, and Feast upon the Cream, which they skim from the Milk.

What kind of Money is currant in the Kingdome of *Fairies*, is not recorded in the Story. But the *Ecclesiastiques* in their Receipts accept of the same Money that we doe; though when they are to make any Payment, it is in Canonizations, Indulgences, and Masses.

To this, and such like resemblances between the *Papacy*, and the Kingdome of *Fairies*, may be added this, that as the *Fairies* have no existence, but in the Fancies of ignorant people, rising from the Traditions of old Wives, or old Poets: so the Spirituall Power of the *Pope* (without the bounds of his own Civill Dominion) consisteth onely in the Fear that Seduced people stand in, of their Excommunication; upon hearing of false Miracles, false Traditions, and false Interpretations of the Scripture.

It was not therefore a very difficult matter, for Henry 8. by his Exorcisme; nor for Qu. Elizabeth by hers, to cast them out. But who knows that this Spirit of Rome, now gone out, and walking by Missions through the dry places of China, Japan, and the Indies, that yeeld him little fruit, may not return, or rather an Assembly of Spirits worse than he, enter, and inhabite this clean swept house, and make the End thereof worse than the Beginning? For it is not the Romane Clergy onely, that pretends the Kingdome of God to be of this World, and thereby to have a Power therein, distinct from that of the Civill State. And this is all I had a designe to say, concerning the Doctrine of the POLITIQUES. Which when I have reviewed, I shall willingly expose it to the censure of my Countrey.